Side by Side
Audio Writing Workshops

Language
Network

McDougal Littell
A HOUGHTON MIFFLIN COMPANY
Evanston, Illinois • Boston • Dallas

ISBN 0-618-05340-9

1 2 3 4 5 6 7 8 9 – BHV – 04 03 02 01 00

Contents

Inside *Side by Side:*
How to Use These Materials

As an English teacher today, you may be asked to operate successfully in a multicultural, multilingual classroom. Although this diversity offers exciting opportunities for students to learn from one another, it can complicate your task of helping each student learn to communicate clearly. It is not easy both to challenge the most fluent native speaker of English in your class and to provide support for the student who is struggling with English.

You are already using *Language Network* to help you teach grammar, writing, and communication skills. These *Side by Side* materials can help you give students acquiring English (also known as English as a Second Language students, or ESL) the support that will enable them to develop their writing skills and to complete the same assignments as their classmates who are native speakers of English. Like *Language Network,* these materials are based on the conviction that writing is a way of discovering and exploring ideas, that all students have worthwhile ideas to share, and that by working side by side with one another, all students can become successful writers.

The materials in the *Side by Side* books will enable you to help your students acquiring English write persuasively, develop a compelling narrative, and complete the other guided assignments in *Language Network.* Following is a detailed description of the components of this package and suggestions on how to incorporate them into your teaching.

Teacher's Notes

The Teacher's Notes include ideas for preparing students to write, answers to the student model questions, strategies for helping students work through each step in the writing assignment, and options for assessment. Suggestions for grouping students for cooperative activities, presenting vocabulary, and tailoring reading and writing activities to individual proficiency levels are included on pages 3–12 of this book and are referenced at appropriate places in the Teacher's Notes.

Using the Teacher's Notes.   Before beginning a lesson, you might want to review the Teacher's Notes and decide which strategies will help you meet your students' needs and how you will apply them.

Compact Disk

The CD introduces each type of writing and leads students step by step through each writing assignment. Students are given concrete instructions about what they should do at each stage of the process—listen to the CD, pause the CD and do an activity, or consult with their teacher or classmates. The material presented orally on the CD is also available in the written script for each lesson. It is suggested that you photocopy the script and have students follow along as they listen to the CD.

Using the CD.   Explain to students that the CD will help them complete their writing assignment successfully. Make sure students know how to use the CD

- Give a copy of the script and copies of the worksheets to each student.

- Direct students to listen to the CD and to read the script as they listen.

- Tell students to follow the instructions on the CD for each step of the assignment. Reassure them that the CD will explain how they are to use the worksheets and that they can pause the CD at any time and ask you or another student for help.

Script

The script is a transcript of the CD. By photocopying it so that students can follow along as they listen to the CD, you will provide them with visual input that will help them understand what they hear. They can to refer to the script for clarification during their writing process and for review later.

Using the script.   To prepare yourself for each lesson, you might want to review the script instead of listening to the CD. On your copy, you might highlight vocabulary words and any concepts that you want to present to students before they begin the writing assignment.

Worksheets

Several worksheets accompany each lesson. Other worksheets help students to find, develop, and organize ideas and to reflect on their writing. The CD includes specific instructions that will enable students to complete the worksheets and incorporate the information into their writing.

Using the worksheets.   Before students begin the lesson, make sure that each has copies of the accompanying worksheets. The CD instructs students to confer with you at various points in the lesson—usually before beginning activities and after completing worksheets. You will probably want to check their completed worksheets routinely and to have them check in with you at other points that are suggested in the Teacher's Notes or that you think appropriate.

The Foundations of *Side by Side:*
Understanding Students Acquiring English and Helping Them to Write

Students acquiring English bring to the classroom a rich variety of experiences and diverse language, academic, and social skills. Some may have had extensive schooling in their countries of origin. Others come with little schooling but may have had experiences that matured them far beyond their years. How can you address this diversity in your classroom? How can you involve students in meaningful writing activities even if their English is limited?

Understanding How Students Acquiring English Learn

Although students acquiring English go through the same learning process as native English-speaking students, they face additional problems specific to second-language learning. Following are some basic premises that can help you tailor your teaching to meet your students' needs.

Acquisition of English comes from real use.   Students learn language and other skills naturally and holistically as they attempt to make sense of the world around them. An activity-oriented classroom, one in which students are frequently allowed to collaborate in or direct their own learning process, provides an atmosphere that promotes this type of natural learning. Since students are active partners in such a classroom, they can start from what they already know and seek out information in accordance with their personal and social needs. Classroom activities that give students acquiring English many reasons and opportunities to use English can help develop their confidence and skill.

Experience is central to the learning process for students acquiring English.   The personal experiences that students acquiring English bring to the classroom are a valuable resource that teachers can use to develop their students' language skills. Such instructional activities as small-group discussion, response to stories and poems, and the use of journals and learning logs can motivate students to explore and communicate their personal experiences. By doing so, they will also be practicing and strengthening both oral and written language skills. They must constantly do, say, and write to anchor and integrate their developing knowledge of English.

Opportunities to share their cultures can enhance students' feelings of self-worth.   While experiencing the same personal, social, and academic problems as their classmates, students acquiring English often have the added difficulty of feeling like outsiders. The respect that you and their classmates show to these students can bolster their confidence and help them learn. The following kinds of support can reinforce students' pride in their native languages and cultures as they develop fluency in English:

- allowing students to use their native languages during prewriting

- motivating students to explore and share aspects of their native languages and cultures orally and in writing

- pairing students with bilingual classmates

- inviting students' parents to observe or speak to the class

Reasonable expectations and assessment standards can encourage students to experiment with English yet allow them to succeed.   Students acquiring English will make many mistakes as they learn the language. You can encourage them to experiment with English by allowing them to use any methods that will help them communicate, such as drawings, "temporary" spellings, and idiosyncratic syntax. Try to correct only those errors that interfere with meaning, since the correct forms will gradually emerge as students gain experience with the language. The more opportunities students have to hear and read English and to speak and write it themselves, the more quickly they will develop fluency.

Applying Specific Teaching Strategies

You can help your students acquiring English to engage in meaningful writing activities in several different ways. Your efforts to understand their needs and to provide a supportive classroom atmosphere are an important first step. In addition, you can encourage these students to write by helping them work cooperatively with others and by using specific strategies to teach comprehension, vocabulary, reading, and writing.

Developing Cooperative-Learning Skills

Using cooperative-learning strategies is a good way to help students develop social, academic, and communication skills. This student-centered instructional approach is particularly effective in involving students acquiring English in classroom activities and in the teaching of writing. When cooperative learning is used for writing activities, it provides students with many opportunities to exchange ideas and cultural perspectives while practicing English.

Grouping students acquiring English for cooperative learning.   Groups of four students are ideal for cooperative learning, and each group can be easily split into pairs for other activities. Students can be grouped to accommodate individual needs or to meet the requirements of a particular activity. For example, a new immigrant or a particularly shy student could be paired with a bilingual "buddy" for both cooperative and individual activities. The buddies should be advised that their task is to help the students acquiring English do activities themselves, not to do the activities for them. You could also group four students with the same primary language background for tasks, such as prewriting activities, that are accomplished most effectively in the students' primary language. In general, however, heterogeneous grouping is most effective, since it teaches all students to deal with diversity and to develop other important interactive skills.

Preparing students for cooperative learning.   You can establish a climate of cooperation by making sure that students understand the rules that govern cooperative activities and by modeling and having students role-play positive and negative behaviors. For example, students must learn that they can best help each other not by providing answers but by leading their peers to discover answers for themselves. This type of peer response can be especially helpful to students acquiring English and can be used at all stages of the writing process.

The following conversation is an example of good peer response:

SAE: Here it says that I have to write a topic sentence. What is the answer?

Peer: There is no right answer. A topic sentence tells the main idea of your paper, and you should write one in your first draft. What are you writing about?

SAE: About a beautiful city by the ocean.

Peer: Look at your first sentence. Does it show that main idea?

SAE: "The town was big." I don't think that shows the idea. Do you?

Peer: No, not really. What else could you say to show the idea of a beautiful city by the ocean?

SAE: How about "I had never seen so many tall glass buildings before"?

Peer: That's great. It gives me a good picture of the city and makes me want to read more.

To ensure that students are comfortable with a cooperative activity, make sure that they fully understand what process they will go through. Explain the materials and resources they are to use, and write on the board the step-by-step procedure they should follow. Be sure to enumerate the specific skills—thinking, listening, speaking, reading, writing, and interactive—that will be used in the activity, the form that students' final products should take, and the criteria on which their performance will be evaluated. Whenever possible, give instructions both orally and in writing. In their groups, students should then discuss what role each member will have, how to begin their task, what resources to use, how to present their work, and how to evaluate both their process and their final product.

Using cooperative strategies. The following activities can be done by students working in pairs or groups of four:

- **Two-minute workout** Students turn to their neighbors and for two minutes, discuss, write, or draw their ideas about a given topic. This technique works well to foster fluency and generate ideas for writing.

- **Brainstorming** Students list as many ideas or facts about or associations with a particular topic as they can. Like the two-minute workout, this technique fosters fluency and can be used at almost any stage of reading or writing.

- **Round table** Students sit in a circle. One writes a sentence or two and passes the paper to the next student. That student adds another sentence or two and passes the paper along. The procedure continues, with each student adding to what has already been written. This technique can be used for retelling stories, for summarizing material, or for collaborative writing.

- **Jigsaw** A writing or other learning task is divided into four parts. Each student on a team is responsible for doing one part of the task and for working with the other students to create a unified product. For example, writing about causes and effects could be divided into the following four tasks: researching the causes, researching the effects, picking the most important causes and effects to focus on, and developing an organizational scheme. All four students could then collaborate on the writing.

Monitoring cooperative learning. As students engage in cooperative activities, carefully observe and record the group interactions. Note both individual participation and performance and the effectiveness of the group as a whole. Your records can provide evidence of students' progress in social skills and in written and oral language skills. You can discuss your observations with students and ask them to evaluate their own experiences. Questions they might ask themselves include, What did we do? How did we do it? Why did we do it? What did we learn? How can we use what we learned? and, How did I feel about the experience? To give students writing practice, you might ask them to record their answers to these questions.

Developing Comprehension

Students develop oral and written language skills concurrently. You can use verbal and nonverbal techniques to help your students acquiring English understand spoken English. These techniques will also help them understand what they read and can help them improve their writing. Approaches you can try include using your own speech patterns as a model, asking specific kinds of questions, and embedding new information in a concrete and familiar context.

Using your own speech as a model. The way you use English in the classroom can make the language easier for students acquiring English to understand and serve as a model they can mimic. The following specific techniques can be helpful:

- Speak at a slow but natural rate.

- Enunciate clearly.

- Use simple, short sentences.

- Repeat statements slowly a few times, then, if necessary, rephrase and clarify them.

- Write (or illustrate) vocabulary, idioms, and concepts on the board.

- Give specific instructions and write them on the board.

- Break down complex tasks into simple steps.

Asking the right questions. The kinds of conversations and questions that are most helpful to students acquiring English are ones that encourage them to provide information. Specific techniques include the following:

- Engage students in dialogue as much as possible.

- Make conversations concrete and personal rather than abstract.

- Question students frequently, using a variety of strategies, such as

—*wh-* questions *(who, what, where, when, why)*

—"proof" questions ("How do you know that?" "What makes you think so?")

—"trick" questions ("The head of the United States is called a king, right?")

—confirmation checks ("Do you mean . . .?")

- Ask questions that are legitimate requests for new information ("What do you think this looks like?") rather than ones to which you already know the answers ("Where is the boy?").

- Use a positive technique, such as restatement, to correct errors (Student: "Does she has a pet?" Teacher: "Does she *have* a pet? Yes, she does. Yes, she has a pet.").

Embedding new information in familiar contexts.   All students learn best when new information is presented in a way that relates it to what they already know. Some verbal and nonverbal approaches that you can try include the following:

- using concrete examples that students are familiar with

- providing nonverbal reinforcement with

  —pantomime, gestures, and facial expressions
  —props and real objects
  —pictures, photographs, and blackboard sketches
  —films, filmstrips, videotapes, slides, and transparencies
  —demonstrations, skits, and role-playing
  —hands-on, interactive tasks

Developing Vocabulary

A classroom atmosphere that helps students learn and remember new vocabulary will greatly enhance their language development. The following strategies can be helpful:

- providing a language-rich environment filled with print materials and opportunities for reading, writing, listening, and speaking

- promoting an interactive, cooperative forum in which students' ideas are solicited, respected, and used as the basis for discussion

- correcting mistakes in a way that supports students' communicative efforts and encourages them to try again

Strategies such as illustrating verbal material visually and presenting new words in contexts that students are familiar with can also contribute to vocabulary development.

Providing nonverbal support for vocabulary acquisition. Visual images, sounds, and actions can all assist students in forming associations that will help them remember new words. Suggest that students try any or all of the following activities when presented with new words:

- mentally picture or actually draw an image related to a word, or write the word down

- identify a word in their own language that sounds like the new word

- physically act out a concrete concept, such as heaviness, or role-play a situation depicting an abstract concept, such as betrayal

Helping students integrate and apply new vocabulary. Various techniques can help students make new words part of their active vocabularies. You should first model a technique, talking through the process as you do it, and then have students practice it, either alone or in groups. These techniques include the following:

- **Mapping** Using semantic maps, word webs, Venn diagrams, and other cognitive organizers enables students to make varied associations with new words. Encourage students to use drawings for words not yet in their repertoire. Here is an example of a word web or semantic map:

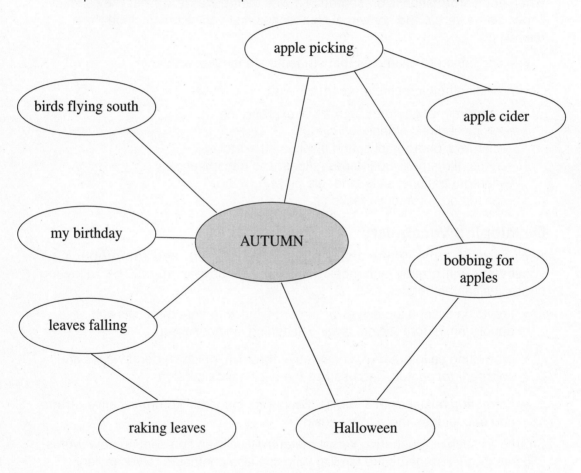

- **Grouping and classifying** This technique enables students to add on new words and concepts to their existing knowledge and conceptual structures. Words can be grouped into categories by

　—part of speech (nouns, pronouns, verbs)
　—topic (words about weather)

—practical function (words for parts of a computer)
—semantic function (words linked by similarity or dissimilarity of meaning)
—linguistic function (words used in apologizing, requesting, denying)

- **Creating word banks** Students should keep records of the new words they learn, perhaps by writing the words on cards color-coded for various categories. They can use their word banks for individual or cooperative language activities, such as revising and editing their writing and conducting spelling bees.

- **Writing "meaningful" sentences** Students can fix the meanings of new words in their minds by using the words in sentences that give clues to their meanings. For example, the following sentence illustrates the meaning of the word *agree:* "I'm sure you'll *agree* to eat at Hamburger Heaven because you like hamburgers and French fries." You might suggest that students create a meaningful sentence for each word that they include in their word banks.

- **Using dictionaries and thesauruses** These reference books can be very helpful to students acquiring English. Encourage students, however, to try to use context clues to figure out the meanings of unfamiliar words that they hear or read before they look the words up in a dictionary. They can also consult dual-language dictionaries. You might want to suggest that students share each word, its definition, and perhaps a corresponding meaningful sentence with the class.

- **Highlighting** You can help students remember vocabulary words or key concepts by calling attention to them visually. Techniques such as writing with colored chalk, underlining, or drawing boxes or circles around items can be helpful.

- **Keeping learning logs** Learning logs can help students develop their vocabularies by providing a place for them to record

  —vocabulary words, definitions, and meaningful sentences
  —unfamiliar words or concepts
  —personal thoughts, feelings, goals, and objectives
  —personal problems and possible solutions
  —learning strategies found to be successful

A learning log can also be a rich source of writing ideas.

Developing Reading Skills

Like oral and written language skills, reading and writing skills often develop simultaneously. Offering opportunities for students acquiring English to use a variety of strategies to read many different English materials can increase their fluency, comprehension, and enjoyment of the language. In turn, their writing will benefit.

Providing a framework for reading. You can provide the following general types of language support as students gain experience with reading and writing in English:

- Prepare students for reading by eliciting prior knowledge and providing background and vocabulary support.

- If possible, edit selections so that students will read only key paragraphs.

- Highlight important information and key vocabulary.

- Encourage students to ask questions and to share their personal reactions to reading selections orally.

- "Think aloud" as you read, modeling comprehension, inference, and prediction.

- Form cooperative pairings or teams to enhance students' study of vocabulary and other language skills.

- Have students use patterns and vocabulary from reading selections to create their own writing.

- During drafting and revision, emphasize language development rather than right answers and correct grammar. This will help students develop confidence and enable them to become comfortable with peer response and with editing.

- Set high but flexible standards.

- Develop appropriate rubrics specifically for assessing these students' writing.

Implementing specific reading strategies.   Techniques that you can have students either use successively as their skills increase or apply as appropriate to different reading selections include the following:

- following along silently in the text as you read aloud

- reading aloud softly with you

- reading alternate sentences aloud with partners who are native speakers of English, discussing the selections as they read, and summarizing the selections after they have finished

- reading silently

Involving students in activities that can help them absorb what they have read.   Language activities that can help students learn from and remember what they read include the following:

- discussing with partners or cooperative-team members what they have learned

- answering questions about selections

- mapping story lines or illustrating characters, settings, or plot elements

- acting out scenes from selections

- finding out the meanings of unfamiliar words

- practicing the pronunciations and spellings of new words

- writing in their journals or learning logs

Developing Writing Skills

Writing is a skill much more difficult for students acquiring English to master than listening, speaking, and reading. Nevertheless, don't wait until students have perfected other language skills to have them write. In fact, the sooner students begin writing, the faster their overall fluency in English will improve.

Offering motivation and encouragement. Students' initial attempts at writing will likely be imperfect and full of errors. You can encourage them by responding positively to what they are trying to say and by working with them to clarify their ideas. Try to focus on their ideas and on the things they have done right—for example, at first you might want to correct only errors that affect meaning.

Students acquiring English should be given the same writing assignments as other students; but the instructions must be clear and simple, and your expectations should be tailored to each student's degree of English proficiency. You might want to limit early assignments to one paragraph each and to ignore grammar and mechanics. This will enable you to analyze students' writing and to work out an individualized plan for each student.

Providing writing support. There are several kinds of support you can offer students acquiring English to help them improve their writing skills. Try any or all of the following approaches:

- Make available a variety of reading materials that students can understand and enjoy.

- Engage students in kinds of prewriting activities—such as discussion, brainstorming, and drawing—that enable them to explore new vocabulary and concepts.

- Encourage students to discuss and share their writing with others.

- Allow students to write cooperatively in pairs or small teams.

- Respond constructively to students' work by reinforcing their ideas and correcting only selected kinds of errors. (Make sure that students understand which errors you will focus on, however.)

Assessing Writing from Students Acquiring English

In addition to receiving input from you and their classmates on their writing, students acquiring English should engage in critical evaluation of their own writing from the beginning. To assess your students, you might want to use the three-step rubric described in the following sections, defining the levels specifically to meet the criteria of each assignment. This rubric can also help you foster students' proofreading skills and enable them to evaluate their own writing.

Establishing writing expectations. The following general definitions of competency levels may help you formulate your expectations for specific writing assignments:

- **Level 1—Novice** Students often incorporate English words into the syntax of their primary languages. Writing skills in their primary languages may be limited.

For these students, a reasonable expectation for descriptive writing might be a short paragraph, perhaps accompanied by a drawing. A persuasive piece might consist of two or three paragraphs of perhaps three sentences each. You might want to provide a template for the overall structure of the paper and to provide students with sentence openings, such as "I believe . . ." and "The first reason I believe this is . . ." Students should be allowed to use dual-language dictionaries and to work closely with peers who are native speakers of English.

- **Level 2—Basic**   Students are able to produce complete, but possibly choppy, sentences. They make many mechanical and grammatical errors and may use "temporary" spellings and syntax. They demonstrate a basic knowledge of English structures, though their writing may occasionally include words in their primary languages.

  These students can be expected to produce two or three expository paragraphs with few errors that impede meaning. Their persuasive writing should consist of several two- or three-sentence paragraphs and should show an awareness of the appropriate use of evidence and support.

- **Level 3—Intermediate**   Students are able to produce complete sentences and generally coherent paragraphs. Their writing lacks style and creativity, however.

  These students should be given many examples of expository and persuasive writing to read and use as models. Their writing should contain no errors that impede meaning and only a limited number of grammatical and mechanical errors. It should also show evidence of unity and coherence.

Students whose competency exceeds the intermediate level are able to produce fluent prose that expresses their ideas clearly and may show evidence of creativity. The writing produced by these students can be judged by the same standards you apply to your native English-speaking students.

Fostering proofreading skills.   Initially, students acquiring English might just read other students' work and watch them edit and proofread. After a time, you can have the students acquiring English focus on one or two specific aspects of grammar or mechanics and disregard other errors.

Here are types of errors you can expect to be made by students of various ability levels and the corresponding proofreading strategies to suggest:

- **Level 1—Novice**

  Frequent errors—wrong words; incorrect tenses; misspellings; misuses of articles, adjectives, and connecting words; and incorrect syntax
  Proofreading strategies—Help students correct misspellings, incorrect uses of words, and syntactical problems that affect meaning (for example, "Football likes me"). Stress accurate expression of ideas, not extensive development.

- **Level 2—Basic**

  Frequent errors—limited vocabulary, misuses of transitional words and of punctuation, incorrect sentence structures, and lack of coherence

Proofreading strategies—Help students correct wrong or missing punctuation, repetition of words, and incorrect sentence structures (for example, "It raining"). Stress coherent development of ideas, not elegance of expression.

Level 3—Intermediate

Frequent errors—mechanical, grammatical, and syntactic errors similar to those of native English speakers who are inexperienced writers; unclear focus and insufficient development and support of ideas

Proofreading strategies—Help students correct all mechanical and grammatical errors and improve overall unity and cohesion. Stress development of creativity and style.

English is the second (or third or fourth) language for these students, and they initially filter information through their native tongues. However, with your encouragement and support, and by working side by side with their classmates and using materials tailored to their needs, students acquiring English will learn to write clearly in English on topics they care about.

Glossary for Writers

The following terms related to the writing process not only can help students complete their writing assignments but can also enrich their vocabularies and help them understand what they read. You might want to photocopy these pages and have students keep copies for future reference.

argument—speech or writing that states an opinion and gives reasons to support it

assessment—a judgment or rating. A grade of B+ and a four-star movie rating are examples of assessments.

audience—readers or listeners. For example, your teacher and classmates will probably be the audience for most of the writing you do in school.

brainstorming—a way of finding ideas by listing all things that come to mind without stopping to judge them. Brainstorming can help you at almost any stage of the writing process—from finding a topic to choosing a way to publish your work.

chronological order—time order; the order in which things happen

collaboration—working with other people to share ideas and solve problems

comparison and contrast—explaining two or more ideas or things by showing how they are alike and how they are different

controversial issue—an issue that causes strong disagreement

controversy—a strong disagreement

description—a picture created with words

detail—a specific piece of information about a person, place, or thing

dialogue—a spoken or written conversation between two or more people

drafting—the stage of the writing process in which you put your ideas on paper. Writers usually make several drafts before they are satisfied with their work.

elaboration—presenting reasons, examples, and details to support an idea

essay—a group of paragraphs focused on a topic

example—an instance or illustration: the Fourth of July is an example of an American holiday.

freewriting—a way of exploring ideas, thoughts, or feelings by writing whatever comes into your mind for a certain period of time. Since no one else needs to see your freewriting, you can let your ideas flow freely, without worrying about correct language or grammar.

idea tree—a drawing in which a main idea is shown on the trunk of a tree and related ideas are shown on the branches

journal—a notebook in which a person writes about personal thoughts, feelings, problems, and events

main idea—the most important idea

narrative—a story

narrator—the person who tells a story

opinion—a judgment or belief about someone or something

paragraph—a group of sentences about a subject; usually contains a topic sentence stating the main idea of the paragraph

peer response—suggestions or comments provided by your classmates at any stage of the writing process. Comments such as "I like the way you begin this story; it makes me want to read on" and "I'm not sure what you mean here; can you tell me more?" are examples of helpful peer response.

persuasion—writing done to convince readers to believe or act a certain way

point of view—the perspective from which a story is told. In first-person point of view, the narrator is a character in the story and uses pronouns like *I* and *me.* In third-person point of view, the narrator is not a character and uses pronouns like *he, she, him,* and *her.*

prewriting—the stage of the writing process in which you explore ideas and begin gathering information. Prewriting can be done in your head, out loud, or in writing.

proofreading—the stage of the writing process in which you check what you have written for errors in capitalization, spelling, and grammar and correct any errors that you find

publishing—the stage of the writing process in which you share your completed writing with other people

quotation—words repeated from a conversation or a piece of literature. For example, in writing about Doris Lessing's story "A Sunrise on the Veld," a student used a quotation from the story in this way: *The boy considers shooting the buck to end its misery but decides not to, saying, "I can't stop it. I can't stop it. There's nothing I can do."*

reason—a statement telling why an opinion seems right

revising—the stage of the writing process in which you think about what you have written and change it to make it better

sensory details—pieces of information showing how something looks, smells, sounds, tastes, or feels

spatial order—the order in which things are arranged in space—for example, from inside to outside or from top to bottom

subject—a topic being discussed or written about

summarize—to state ideas in a brief way. For example, you could summarize a person's life by saying that he or she was born, grew up, grew old, and died.

support—backing up an opinion with facts and examples

tone—the feeling created by a piece of writing. A piece of writing might have, for example, a serious, sad, or angry tone.

topic—the subject of a piece of writing or a speech

transition—a word or phrase that connects sentences or paragraphs to show how ideas are related. For example, the transition *on the other hand* is used to introduce an idea that is unlike the idea that came before.

transition words—words that show how ideas are connected to one another

voice—the way a writer or speaker uses diction, sentence structure, and figurative language to create a unique "sound" in written or spoken text

word map or web—a drawing in which words are circled and connected with lines to show how ideas are related. A word map or web can be a way of exploring a topic or of finding supporting details and examples.

Writing Process

Thinking Skills for Writing

Arrange the steps of the writing process in the correct order.

✂ -

(a) **Think about what you have learned:** Think about the problems you had writing this paper and how you solved them. What would you do differently next time?

- -

(b) **Write a draft:** At this point, you want to write down your ideas on paper. Don't worry about being perfect now. You can change things around later if you want to.

- -

(c) **Pick a topic:** Choose a writing topic that interests you. To help you think of ideas, you can make lists of things you like. For example, list sports, hobbies, or holidays you like. Then, choose the idea that you like best.

- -

(d) **Revise your first draft:** Read your draft over and ask a friend to read it, too. Think about ways to make your writing clearer.

- -

(e) **Collect details about your topic:** Think about what your audience needs to know in order to understand what you plan to write about. Then explore your topic. Write down all the details about it. One good way to do this is to use a web diagram.

- -

(f) **Edit and proofread your revised draft:** Continue changing your writing until you feel that it is clear and interesting. Then, check your grammar, punctuation, and spelling. After you have made all your changes, make a clean copy of your paper.

- -

(g) **Organize your paper:** Think about how you will organize the information you have found. Then, talk to your teacher about how you will present your ideas.

Sequential Paragraph

Thinking Skills for Writing

Arrange the sentences of each paragraph in the appropriate order.

✂ Paragraph 1

1(a) Finally, you average the numbers and come up with a rating for the movie.

1(b) Next, you rate the acting on a scale of 1–10.

1(c) I thought of a great new way to rate movies.

1(d) First, you rate the plot on a scale of 1–10.

Paragraph 2

2(a) But before you get to Harrisburg, get on Route 76, which will take you straight to Pittsburgh.

2(b) Let me explain the best route to get to Pittsburgh.

2(c) From York, catch Route 83 towards Harrisburg.

2(d) Then, go around the city of Lancaster and drive to York.

2(e) The first thing to do to get to Pittsburgh is to drive toward Lancaster.

Cause and Effect Paragraph

Thinking Skills for Writing

Arrange the sentences of each paragraph in the appropriate order.

✂ **Paragraph 1**

1(a) Then, my mother starts thinking that the grass has grown too high and needs to be cut.

1(b) And that doesn't make me happy because I have to spend all Saturday afternoon mowing the lawn!

1(c) The warm weather makes our grass grow fast.

1(d) Every March, the weather gets warm and rainy.

1(e) So she asks me to mow it.

Paragraph 2

2(a) According to one theory, a huge asteroid fell from space.

2(b) This left meat-eating dinosaurs without food, and they died of hunger, too.

2(c) As a result, plant-eating animals died of hunger.

2(d) Scientists are still trying to explain why dinosaurs disappeared millions of years ago.

2(e) Without sunlight, many plants died.

2(f) The asteroid's impact created a dust cloud so big that sunlight did not reach Earth's surface.

Comparison-Contrast Paragraph   *Thinking Skills for Writing*

Arrange the sentences of each paragraph in the appropriate order.

✂ **Paragraph 1**

- -

1(a) Independence Day, on the other hand, is a national holiday in the United States.

- -

1(b) It is celebrated on May 5th, the day the battle of Puebla was won.

- -

1(c) I will compare two national holidays, Cinco de Mayo and Independence Day.

- -

1(d) It is celebrated on July 4th, the day America declared its independence.

- -

1(e) So, both days are holidays celebrating freedom, but they are on different dates because of their historical roots.

- -

1(f) Let's start with Cinco de Mayo, a national holiday in Mexico.

- -

Paragraph 2

- -

2(a) Crocodiles and alligators seem like similar reptiles.

- -

2(b) So, although they are alike in many ways, alligators and crocodiles are different reptiles.

- -

2(c) Alligators have shorter and rounder noses than crocodiles.

- -

2(d) To begin, both animals have long bodies and scaly skin.

- -

2(e) Another difference is that alligators can live in cooler climates than crocodiles.

- -

2(f) They also spend time a lot of time in water. So, how are they different?

Five-Paragraph Composition

Thinking Skills for Writing

Arrange the five paragraphs in the appropriate order.

✂ --

(a) When we got home, we were both very happy. This trip brought us back together again. Now, although I am sad to see him leave for college soon, I am not worried. I know that my brother will always be my best friend.

(b) From Montana, we stopped at Yellowstone National Park. We sat waiting for "Old Faithful," an amazing geyser that shoots water up into the air once every hour. My brother asked a ranger to take a picture of us standing in front of the gushing water.

(c) The first place we visited was Glacier National Park in Montana. My brother explained that a glacier is a river of ice. It moves so slowly that you can't tell it's moving. He took me on a hike in the park. On the way back, he carried my backpack because I was very tired.

(d) Last summer, I went on a trip with my older brother. It was the first chance we had to spend time together since he had left for college. We decided to go visit some national parks and monuments.

(e) On the way home from Yellowstone, we went to South Dakota to see Mount Rushmore. The artist Gutzon Borglum made an enormous sculpture there, carved right out of the side of a mountain. It shows the heads of four American presidents. I told my brother that maybe his head would be carved there someday. That made him laugh.

Introductions

Arrange the sentences of each introduction in the appropriate order.

✂ **Paragraph 1**

- -

1(a) Then, I will examine two main sources: inventions and other languages.

- -

1(b) In this essay, I will show that new words, such as *chat room* or *sushi,* come from different sources.

- -

1(c) Have you ever wondered where new words come from?

- -

Paragraph 2

- -

2(a) But most importantly, it has changed the way we communicate with each other around the world.

- -

2(b) The World Wide Web is a powerful tool.

- -

2(c) It has changed many things about the way we live and work.

- -

Paragraph 3

- -

3(a) Although formal letter-writing is becoming a lost art, writing casual e-mails helps improve writing and communication skills.

- -

3(b) In the 1700s, people like Thomas Jefferson wrote many long, formal letters by hand every week.

- -

3(c) They do, however, write lots of e-mail messages.

- -

3(d) But today, people write very few letters.

- -

Conclusions

Thinking Skills for Writing

Arrange the sentences of each conclusion in the correct order.

✂ **Paragraph 1**

1(a) And their latest theories give us an idea of the scientific method at work.

1(b) We don't know for sure what caused the dinosaurs to disappear.

1(c) Scientists are looking for evidence to solve this mystery.

Paragraph 2

2(a) But if our entire team tells her about the problem, then she will have to take action.

2(b) Now you understand why this problem is important, and why we must report it to the coach.

2(c) If only a few of us complain, however, the coach will not change anything.

Paragraph 3

3(a) People may dislike spiders because of how they look.

3(b) That is why we should all learn to appreciate and even admire spiders.

3(c) But as this essay shows, most spiders are not only harmless to humans, they are also useful.

Adding Factual Elaboration to a Paragraph

Thinking Skills for Writing

Add to or switch an appropriate fact to each sentence in the paragraph.

✂

[1] A scientist | [1] helped create television in the 1920s.

[2] But broadcasting did not begin in the U.S. | [2] until | [2] later.

[3] Then, scientists made television better | [3] .

[4] Today, | [4] most homes | [4] have at least one TV set.

[5] There are even two Museums of Television and Radio

[5] in America | [5] .

Facts:

[a] 97 million homes in America

[b] , one is in Los Angeles, the other in New York City

[c] after the Second World War.

[d] A Russian-American scientist called Vladimir Zworykin

[e] by making color TVs and introducing cable access

Adding Sensory Elaboration to a Paragraph

Thinking Skills for Writing

Add to or switch an appropriate detail to each sentence of the paragraph.

✂ -

1 When the movie begins, we hear thunder   **1** .

2 Then, we see Count Dracula's castle   **2** .

3 A young man   **3** is riding a horse up the mountain.

4 At dinner, the young man   **4** won't eat his soup   **4** .

5 As the movie goes on, the young man   **5** gets really old.

Details:

a wearing a soft silk cape and rich leather boots

b perched on top of a steep, bare mountain

c becomes wrinkled and his hair thins and grays.

d clapping violently in the night sky

e because it smells like rotten eggs

Adding Incidents, Examples, Quotations

Add the incident, quotation, and example provided to the paragraph below.

1 Some people do not believe teenagers care about the world they live in.

2 But I think that most teenagers are like me. They are serious and care about their communities.

3 There are many other ways in which teenagers get involved to make a better world.

Incident, example, quotation:

a For example, some teach younger children, while others start recycling programs or gather used clothing.

b One way I show that I care is by tending older people's gardens. It started last year, when my friends and I noticed that a garden was looking abandoned. We found out that the owner was sick. So, for two months, we spent our weekends working in the garden. The owner was very happy and thanked us, with tears in his eyes. After that, we started an "SOS Garden" service. Now, in our town, teenage volunteers take care of older peoples' gardens for free.

c These people agree with a French poet who said, "When you are seventeen, you aren't really serious."

Combining Short Sentences

Thinking Skills for Writing

Combine each pair of sentences into one sentence. Use the words and commas provided.

1 Juan likes all kinds of movies   **1** .

1 His favorites are westerns.

1 but   **1** ,

2 He started to watch every western on TV   **2** .

2 He saw his first western and loved it.

2 after

3 They don't make many westerns these days   **3** .

3 He rents videos.

3 ,   **3** so

4 Juan doesn't really like westerns in black and white   **4** .

4 They look so much better in color.

4 because

Combining Sentences Using
Words, Phrases, Appositives

Thinking Skills for Writing

Combine two sentences. Take a word, phrase, or appositive from the second sentence
and add it to the first sentence.

✂

¹ Felipe | ¹ is always telling jokes.

¹ Felipe is | ¹ my best friend | ¹ .

² He started to tell a joke | ² .

² This happened | ² yesterday morning.

³ The joke was about a chicken | ³ .

³ The chicken was | ³ hopping backwards.

⁴ He was about to tell me | ⁴ the punch line | ⁴ .

⁴ The punch line tells

⁴ why the chicken was hopping backwards.

⁵ Just then, Mr. Hernandez | ⁵ called us to the gym.

⁵ He is | ⁵ our coach | ⁵ . | ⁵ , | ⁵ ,

Placement of Modifiers

Add an appropriate modifier to each sentence.

✂

[1] An insect's body   [1] is made up of three   [1] parts:

[1] the head, the thorax, and the abdomen.

[1] different

[2] Insects   [2] have   [2] six legs and two antennae.

[2] always

[3] They use   [3] their   [3] antennae   [3] to feel

[3] the world around them.

[3] sensitive

[4] Some insects,   [4] including flies and bees,   [4] have

[4] wings.   [4] four

[5] A few types of insects   [5] have created

[5] complex societies.   [5] very

Inverted Sentences

Thinking Skills for Writing

Invert the subject and verb in each sentence to make a question.

✂

| [1] Maria | [1] has | [1] seen | [1] the movie you are talking about |

| [1] . | [1] ? |

| [2] That | [2] movie | [2] is | [2] very scary | [2] . | [2] ? |

| [3] The characters | [3] were | [3] really lost in the woods | [3] . |

| [3] ? |

| [4] They | [4] were | [4] looking | [4] for an old cave | [4] . | [4] ? |

| [5] They | [5] did | [5] get | [5] very scared | [5] . | [5] ? |

| [6] They | [6] did | [6] find | [6] their way out | [6] . | [6] ? |

| [7] You | [7] do | [7] think | [7] the actors | [7] will win Oscars |

| [7] . | [7] ? |

Autobiographical Incident

Writing Workshop

In this workshop, you will write about something that has happened to you. You may pause the CD at any time and play it again. You may also ask your teacher or a classmate for help if you do not understand something. When you hear a tone (TONE), pause the CD and follow the instructions.

See How It's Done

When you write about an autobiographical incident, you describe something special that happened to you. Think about a time in your life that was important, such as a birthday or a holiday. Why do you remember that moment?

◆ Turn to Worksheet A. Listen to the first paragraph of one student's description of a special incident in her life. Then, read the rest of Worksheet A on your own. As you read, answer the questions and talk about her writing with your teacher or classmates. (TONE)

Do It Yourself

Elizabeth Kim wrote about understanding something very important about her father. Now it is your turn. Think about things that you have done and things that have happened to you. Choose one experience to write about.

❶ Prewriting ....

Find an idea.

Think about your memories. Write phrases about special times that you remember well. Start each phrase with the words "I was about __ years old when..." You may want to look at old photo albums or read old diaries to help you remember some important times in your life. You can make a life line of your life. Sketch pictures and signs of memories that are important to you.

◆ Fill in Worksheet B with information about events in your life. If you need help, ask your teacher or a classmate. (TONE)

Think about your topic.

Look at your work on Worksheet B. Think about the following questions as you choose a memory to write about:

1. Do I remember enough about this special incident to write about it?
2. Do I feel good about sharing this memory with my classmates and my teacher?
3. Will this incident interest my audience?

◆ Now choose a topic to write about. You may discuss the topic with a classmate or your teacher. (TONE)

Sketch out ideas.

Finding a topic is just the beginning. To help other people understand the incident you chose, you need to sketch out ideas by adding pieces of information.

◆ Fill out Worksheet C with information about your incident. If you need help, ask your teacher or a classmate. (TONE)

Autobiographical Incident

Writing Workshop

❷ Drafting ....

Put your ideas in order.

One way to tell about an incident is to start at the beginning and tell all the events in the order they happened. This kind of order is called **chronological order.** Notice how Elizabeth Kim put the events of her incident in chronological order. Make sure to give enough background information, such as setting and character, as Elizabeth did in the beginning of her second paragraph.

◆ Turn to Worksheet D and fill in the boxes to put your ideas in order. (TONE)

Write a draft of your paper.

Look at all your notes on Worksheets C and D. Take a few minutes to remember your special moment again. Then write down everything you remember in the order it happened. Think about these questions as you write:

1. Does your draft have paragraphs? Remember to start a new paragraph every time something new happens.

2. Does the first paragraph make you want to read more? Is the order clear? Is there enough information?

◆ Now talk with your teacher about how you will present your information and what your finished writing will look like. Then write your draft. (TONE)

❸ Revising ....

Read your draft with a classmate.

When you are ready to show your draft to someone else, read it with a classmate or friend. Another person can help you find ways to make your writing better.

◆ Turn to Worksheet E. Read and answer the questions with your friend or classmate. (TONE)

Change your writing.

Look at your answers on Worksheet E. Can you find places to describe a character in action? Which of the other ideas will make your writing more interesting?

◆ Change your writing to make it better. (TONE)

❹ Editing and Proofreading ....

Proofread your writing and make a final copy.

Meet with your teacher to find out how to proofread your writing for mistakes. After you make the final changes, copy your writing on a clean sheet of paper.

◆ Now proofread your writing and make a clean copy. Put your autobiographical essay in your writing portfolio or folder. (TONE)

❺ Sharing and Reflecting ....

Share your writing and think about what you have learned.

Think about the audience for your autobiographical incident. Will you share it with family or friends? What can you learn from sharing autobiographical writing with others? What did you like or not like about this kind of writing?

◆ Discuss your answers with your teacher and your classmates. (TONE)

For use with Pupil's Edition pp. 404–411

Worksheet A

Writing Workshop

Here is a paper that one student wrote about an incident she remembered. Words and phrases that you may find difficult to understand are underlined and are explained on the right side of the page. As you read, circle any other words you do not understand. First, try to guess their meanings. Then look them up in a dictionary. You may ask your teacher or a classmate for help.

My Father the Dragon
by Elizabeth Kim

1	As a child, I was curious about many <u>aspects</u> of my
2	life. First, I didn't understand why my parents hadn't
3	<u>raised</u> me in Korea, where all my <u>relatives</u> lived. I only
4	knew that my parents immigrated to the United States
5	after they married. Also, I was always curious about the
6	Chinese <u>zodiac</u>, knowing that I am a <u>rooster</u>. When my
7	father told me that he was a <u>dragon</u>, I thought how well
8	the symbol fit him. Later on in my life, I reached an
9	understanding of my parents' hard work and sacrifice to
10	raise a family and of the true meaning of my father's
11	symbol.

aspects–parts

raised–took care of a child
relatives–family members

zodiac–imaginary division of the sky
rooster–adult male chicken
dragon–imaginary monster that breathes fire

? What does this paragraph tell about Elizabeth? Who is she introducing? (TONE)

12	One day when I was about 12 years old, my father
13	came home tired and <u>sore</u> from working hard from six
14	o'clock in the morning to six o'clock at night. He works
15	at a small <u>dry cleaners</u> a block away from our house. Its
16	old, <u>shabby</u> appearance seems almost lost and forgotten
17	behind a new row of stores. On this day, I noticed his
18	hand was <u>bandaged up</u>. He seemed to be in a lot of pain.
19	I felt confused because I always thought of my father as a
20	strong man showing off his <u>biceps</u> and <u>grinning</u> proudly.
21	When I saw my father in pain with bandaged hands, I
22	was surprised. I used to think of him as a dragon–<u>fierce</u>,

sore–hurting

dry cleaners–shop that cleans people's clothes
shabby–old, worn

bandaged up–wrapped with a piece of cloth

biceps–big arm muscles
grinning–smiling

fierce–wild and strong

CHAPTER 18

23 strong, and powerful, just like the zodiac. Suddenly that

24 image faded away as I saw my dad with <u>streaks</u> of white

streaks–lines, stripes

25 in his hair, a frail and overworked body, and injured

26 hands.

> ❓ **What event is Elizabeth writing about? Why does she say it is important to her?**

27   I asked him about his hands, and he told me that he

28 had been fixing machines at the store and cut himself

29 badly. He usually tries to fix everything himself. I asked

30 him, "Why do you have to fix machines when you used

31 to teach math in Korea?" I thought about the black-and-

32 white pictures of his class wearing dark uniforms and my

handsome–good-looking

33 father looking <u>handsome</u> in his suit.

> ✏️ **Underline the details that help describe the main character.**

34   Then my father told me how he had wanted to come

35 to America because he had heard great things about it.

36 He had dreamed of green lawns, picket fences, and

37 friendly neighbors. He had dreamed about <u>vacuums</u> and

vacuums–electrical machines that pick up dust

38 different kinds of machines that would make everything

39 easier. Most of all, he dreamed that his children would

40 grow up in this wonderful country and be happy. He only

41 wanted the best for his children.

> ❓ **What is the main idea of this paragraph?**

42   Then my eyes fell to look at the bandages on his

43 hands, and I didn't see them as a weakness. I saw a

44 whole new picture. My dad was still a dragon inside.

45 This time, however, he had battle wounds. He had

46 sacrificed his high-status job in Korea for his children

47 and came to America, knowing little English. He now

48 works hard in a small cleaners. He cares more deeply

49 about <u>supporting</u> and raising his children in a better

supporting–taking care of children

For use with Pupil's Edition pp. 404–411

Worksheet A (cont.)

50 | environment than he cares about his own health or safety.

51 | He's determined to work hard so that the future of his

52 | children will be better than it would be in Korea.

> **?** **What conclusion does Elizabeth draw from the incident?**

53 | Every day when he comes home from work, I look at

54 | my father proudly. I see a dragon.

> **?** **How does Elizabeth feel about her father?**

Worksheet B

Writing Workshop

On the lines below, complete the phrases to list special times that you remember. Then choose one or two and write as much as you can about each of them on a blank sheet of paper.

1. I was about __ years old when

_____

2. I was about __ years old when

_____

3. I was about __ years old when

_____

4. I was about __ years old when

_____

5. I was about __ years old when

_____

6. I was about __ years old when

_____

7. I was about __ years old when

_____

Draw a life line. Start on the left with your birth. Write important events in your life above the line. Write the date of each event below the line.

my birth

→

19__

For use with Pupil's Edition pp. 404–411

Worksheet C

Writing Workshop

Answer the following questions with as many details as you can about your topic.

Topic: _____

1. When did it happen?

   _____

2. Where did it happen?

   _____

   _____

3. What happened?

   _____

   _____

   _____

   _____

4. Who was there?

   _____

   _____

5. How did I feel?

   _____

   _____

   _____

   _____

6. What did I learn from this incident?

   _____

   _____

   _____

CHAPTER 18

Worksheet D   *Writing Workshop*

Put the events of your incident in the order they happened. Write a short sentence
in each box. You may not need every box, or you may need to add more boxes.

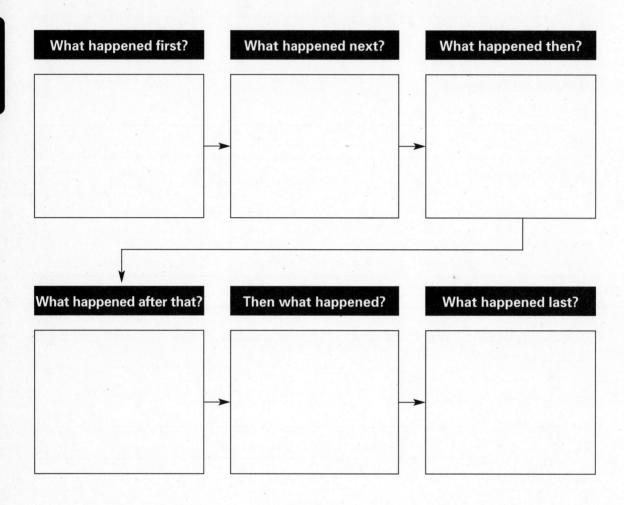

What happened first?

What happened next?

What happened then?

What happened after that?

Then what happened?

What happened last?

When you start writing, the words in this list will help you tell about the order of
the events. These are called transition words.

first	second	then	finally
before	after	next	during
at the beginning	at the same time	at the end	
later	every time	last	
	the next day	soon	
	at that time	always	
	meanwhile		

Worksheet E

Answer these questions with a friend or classmate.

1. Which parts of my writing have enough details? What details can I add to other parts?

_____

_____

_____

_____

2. What words can I add to make the order of events clearer?

_____

_____

_____

3. What information can I add to make it clearer why the event is important to me?

_____

_____

_____

_____

4. Where can I show characters' actions to make the writing more interesting? Are there any words I can change to help show action?

_____

_____

_____

_____

5. Do I clearly tell why this incident was important?

_____

_____

_____

_____

Autobiographical Incident

Background Information

The focus of this workshop is on helping students to convert memorable autobiographical incidents into essays, constructed in chronological order.

Vocabulary for Writing About Literature

Consult pages 7–9 for strategies you may find useful for presenting vocabulary. Make sure that students understand the following terms before they begin this workshop.

autobiographical incident—a special moment that a person has experienced or witnessed

autobiographical essay—a retelling of a personal experience

flashback—a way to add interest by starting at the end or the middle and then going back to the beginning to tell events in order

chronological order—the order that events happen in time; time order

Guiding Your Writers

See How It's Done

- Before students begin the workshop, you may wish to share with them an autobiographical incident of your own or invite them to share examples of authors they have read who have written about autobiographical incidents, either in English or in their native languages.

- Before students turn to Worksheet A, initiate a discussion about the reasons people leave their native countries, as Elizabeth's father did. Talk about the expectations people have when they move to a place like America. You may also want to review the vocabulary in the student model, as well as the following terms:

    immigrated—moved to another country

    symbol—a sign that stands for something

- To ensure comprehension, suggest that students answer the student model questions in pairs or small groups. See page 4 of this booklet for strategies for putting students into pairs or small groups. Invite students to respond to the model.

- **Worksheet A Possible answers:**

    ❓ **What does this paragraph tell about Elizabeth?** she was raised in America; she has family in Korea; she is a rooster in the Chinese zodiac; her father is a dragon in the Chinese zodiac **Who is she introducing?** her father

    ❓ **What event is Elizabeth writing about?** Her father came home one day with bandaged hands. **Why does she say it is important to her?** She saw her father as weak and tired for the first time.

    ✏️ **Underline the details that help describe the main character.** He usually tries to fix everything himself; my father looking handsome in his suit

For use with Pupil's Edition pp. 404–411

Autobiographical Incident

Teacher's Notes

CHAPTER 18

? **What is the main idea of this paragraph?** Her father only wanted the best for his children.

? **What conclusion does Elizabeth draw from the incident?** Her father is still a dragon because he works hard so his children can have a better life.

? **How does Elizabeth feel about her father?** She is proud of him. She thinks he is like a dragon.

Do It Yourself

❶ Prewriting ....

- Explain that students are not limited to the seven phrases on Worksheet B. They may write as many phrases as they can, even using the back of the worksheet if necessary.

- You may want to meet with students individually to discuss the incidents they have decided to write about. Some students may be reluctant to share moments that are private or personal. Explain that they may select a less personal experience or write about an incident that happened to someone else. You may want to review the idea of writing in the third person, with the pronouns *he* and *she* and corresponding verb forms.

- You may want to review students' completed copies of Worksheet C and ask them questions to help them remember additional details.

❷ Drafting ....

- Students may benefit from your giving examples of the use of transitional words and phrases. You may want to recount a shared experience, demonstrating how transition words can help make the order of events clear. Alternatively, you can have students circle or highlight the transition words and phrases in the student model, such as: *Also* (line 5), *Later on* (line 8), and *This time* (line 45).

- If a student has difficulty organizing events, suggest that he or she simply tells a partner what happened. The partner can write down the main parts of the experience in a numbered list.

- Before students begin their drafts, you may suggest one of the following forms to each, according to his or her level of English proficiency:

Option 1
The student writes a paragraph consisting of one sentence for each part of the experience, explaining when and where the experience happened, what happened, who was involved, and how he or she felt during the experience.

Option 2
The student writes a multiparagraph account of the incident, perhaps in the following format:
Paragraph 1
information about the incident, such as when and where it happened.
Paragraph 2–4
a description of the events in the order that they happened

Copyright © McDougal Littell Inc.

For use with Pupil's Edition pp. 404–411

SIDE BY SIDE **41**

Autobiographical Incident

Option 3
The student writes a multiparagraph account in which the flashback technique is used to catch the readers' interest. Any student who decides to include dialogue should be reminded to start a new paragraph each time the speaker changes.

❸ Revising

- Suggest that students read their drafts several times, each time looking for something different. For example, the first reading may focus on the order of the events; the second, on whether characters are shown in action; and the third, on the overall effect of the essay.

- Refer to page 4 for strategies for setting up peer-reader pairs. Suggest that peer readers read the drafts more than once. Be sure that the writers of the drafts understand that they must discuss and answer the questions with their peer readers.

- Emphasize that the writer is the one who decides what will be changed. Ask students to review each suggestion critically to decide whether it will make their writing better.

❹ Editing and Proofreading

- Review with students the process of proofreading. You may want to stress spelling or punctuation rather than capitalization and grammar. Meet with them individually to discuss your expectations for their proofreading. See pages 12–13 for proofreading strategies.

- You may wish to introduce parallel construction as the target skill for this workshop. If students feel confident with their understanding of this skill, you may add parallel construction to their proofreading expectations.

- If students are keeping writing portfolios, suggest that they add their autobiographical essays to their portfolios.

❺ Sharing and Reflecting

- As students reflect on the experience of writing about an autobiographical incident, suggest that they write their answers to the questions before meeting in pairs or small groups to discuss the answers. If students are keeping learning logs, suggest that their answers be included there.

- Initiate a discussion of how autobiographical incidents are often used as bases of short stories, plays, and poems. If students have apprehensions about sharing an autobiographical incident with others, offer suggestions for how they can reach their audience. For example, they may be more comfortable with a poem or short story with a third person narrator.

For use with Pupil's Edition pp. 404–411

Focused Description

Writing Workshop

This CD will help you write a clear description of a person, place, or thing. As you listen to the instructions, pause and replay any parts that are not clear. You might also ask your teacher or another student for help. When you hear a tone (TONE), pause the CD and follow the instructions. Then, start the CD again.

See How It's Done

Look at the things around your classroom. See if you can find an interesting object or person. On a sheet of paper, make a list of the details you would use to describe the object or person to someone who isn't in the room.

◆ Turn to Worksheet A. Listen to the first paragraph of one student's description. Then, continue to read silently on your own. As you read, answer the questions. Discuss them with your teacher or classmate. (TONE)

Do It Yourself

For this assignment, you will write a description of a person, place, or thing that you find interesting. It may be someone you know, a place you like to visit, or an object you own or have seen. The steps that follow will help you carry out the assignment.

❶ Prewriting ....

Think about subjects to write about.

1. Make a list of people, places, or things that have special meaning to you.

2. Make a list of people, places, or things that you find interesting.

◆ Now pause the CD and make these two lists. (TONE)

Choose a subject from your lists of ideas.

Read your lists. What do you want to write about? Think about what interests you and what you think will interest your readers.

◆ Pause the CD and choose a subject to write about. Talk over your choice with your teacher. (TONE)

Collect information about the subject.

Write down details, or pieces of information, about your subject. How does your subject make you feel? How do you want your readers to feel about the person or object? What do your readers already know about your subject? If your subject is a thing, you might want to tell your readers what it can do, how it feels to the touch, and what it sounds and smells like.

◆ Look at the details that Sophie wrote on Worksheet B. Then picture your subject in your mind. Write all the details you can think of to describe it on Worksheet C. (TONE)

❷ Drafting ....

Organize the information you have gathered.

To help your readers form a clear picture of your subject, you need to organize the information. Here are three ways you can arrange the details:

1. Organize the details according to what you see as you look at your subject from left to right, near to far, top to bottom, and so on.

Focused Description

2. Tell what you notice first when you look at the subject, then second, and so on.

3. Write the least important details first, and then write the most important ones.

◆ Look at what you wrote in the first box on Worksheet C. Now take a piece of your own paper and make a list of the details in the order you will write them. Repeat for the other boxes. (TONE)

Get ready to write.

You must plan your draft. Follow these steps to help you complete Worksheet D.

1. Write sentences to tell what you will describe and why it is interesting.

2. Refer to the list you made above to organize the details you will write.

3. Write a sentence that tells how you feel about your subject.

◆ Complete Worksheet D. Then talk with your teacher about what your finished paper will look like. (TONE)

Begin drafting.

As you write, use words that appeal to the senses of sight, sound, smell, and touch. For example, Sophie tells about the "scent of the honey-sweet gardenias." Be sure to use transition words to show the position or location of something.

◆ Now write your first draft. Use the transition words and the sentences you wrote on Worksheet D to help you. (TONE)

❸ Revising ....

Read and revise your writing.

Read your draft. Ask a friend to read it, too. Then discuss the changes you can make. Do your readers get a clear idea of the sights, sounds, and smells you describe?

◆ Turn to Worksheet E. Answer the questions with your friend. (TONE)

❹ Editing and Proofreading ....

Make a final copy.

Are all your sentences complete? Look on page 416 of your book to see how to correct fragments. After you have proofread your writing, make your final copy and share it.

◆ Write your final copy, and then share it with your classmates. (TONE)

❺ Sharing and Reflecting ....

Think about what you have learned in doing this writing.

How is a focused description different from other types of writing? How might you have given your readers a better picture of your subject? How did describing your subject help you remember about it?

◆ Think about these questions. Be ready to share your answers with your teacher and classmates. (TONE)

For use with Pupil's Edition pp. 412–419

Worksheet A

Here is a focused description that a student, Sophie Tyner, wrote. As you read, think about why Sophie chose this place to write about. The underlined words and phrases may be unfamiliar to you. They are explained on the right side of the page. Circle any other words you don't understand and ask your teacher for help.

Far Away, Yet Close to My Heart
by Sophie Tyner

1   My lively, funny grandmother, Doosie, lives in

2   Wahroonga, a quiet underline{suburb} of Sydney, Australia. She has

suburb–small town near a big city

3   occupied the same house for over fifty years. This is my

4   favorite place in the world. Whenever I think of the lush

lush–full of plants

5   gardens by the house, I feel warm and secure.

? **What is Sophie going to write about? Why?** (TONE)

6   Walking down Braeside Street in my memory, I reach

7   number ninety-one and turn onto a curving driveway.

driveway–small road that leads from the street to a house or garage

8   The crunch of gravel under my sandals sounds like

crunch–crackling, crushing sound

9   someone walking in autumn leaves. On my left is a mass

10   of brilliantly colored plants and trees that form a jungle-

11   like barrier between Doosie's land and her neighbors'. To

12   my right is a waist-high stone wall separating the land

waist-high–up to a person's waist

13   from the road. I have often stood on this crumbling wall

14   to reach the lowest branch of a gigantic gum tree. I pull

gum tree–Australian tree

15   myself up and climb high into the thick branches, feeling

16   the bark scrape against my sunburnt arms and legs. After

bark–hard outside covering of a tree
sunburnt–red and burnt by the sun
spongy–soft like a sponge

17   feeling the warm breeze blow through my hair, I slowly

18   climb down and drop to the spongy ground.

? **What does she see on her left? On her right?**

19   I run across the sea of grass and catch the scent of the

20   honey-sweet gardenias in Doosie's front garden. Passing

gardenias–tropical trees with big flowers
hardly–rarely, not often

21   the front door, which is hardly used any more, I unstrap

22   my sandals and toss them onto the waiting step. The heat

Worksheet A (cont.)

23 | is intense, and to escape I <u>duck</u> <u>beneath</u> a branch draped

duck–lower one's body quickly
beneath–under

24 | with ivy. I drink up the coolness of the shade and pause

25 | for a moment to watch a pair of tiny lizards disappear

26 | behind a rock covered with <u>moss</u>. I continue down the

moss–small green plant that grows on trees and rocks
packed–made firm

27 | hidden side path, once <u>packed</u> smooth with the footprints

28 | of my mother and her four brothers as children. The path

29 | leads back to the driveway, curving behind the house. I

30 | <u>amble</u> down it once again, hearing my grandmother's

amble–walk slowly

31 | chattering voice through the kitchen windows. On either

32 | side of the driveway is a sea of bright blue <u>hydrangeas</u>

hydrangeas–plants with large round groups of flowers

33 | that smell as sweet as freshly pressed apple cider.

✎ **Underline the details that tell about what Sophie smells. Circle what she hears.**

34 | Suddenly, I see a flash of black as Doosie's cat Sooty

35 | runs across the hot gravel. I turn and follow her, picking

36 | my way through the <u>gnarly</u> bushes. I feel like <u>Alice in</u>

gnarly–twisted
Alice in Wonderland–book by Lewis Carroll about the adventures of a little girl in a fantastic land

37 | <u>Wonderland</u> as I reach the back garden. Doosie rents this

38 | land now, but I still enjoy coming here. I remember when

39 | I was younger, the garden had flowers so bright your eyes

40 | hurt to look at them. The new <u>tenants</u> do not take care of

tenants–people who rent a house or land

41 | the garden, but it still has its wild beauty. I climb over a

42 | rotting <u>tree stump</u> and run down the slight decline.

✎ **Underline the words that describe how the garden is different now.**

tree stump–part of a tree that is left when the tree is cut down

43 | After glancing at the refreshing blue pools of Doosie's

44 | neighbors, I continue into the old tennis court. It is now

45 | unused and resembles a tiny field. I can easily imagine

46 | my mother with her friends on a hot Australian day

47 | playing tennis. Now the grass court is covered with

prickle–sting

48 | yellow weeds that <u>prickle</u> my bare legs. I gaze at the

❓ **What is Sophie describing in this paragraph?**

49 | garden once more and turn to walk back to the house.

For use with Pupil's Edition pp. 412–419

CHAPTER 19

Worksheet A (cont.)

Writing Workshop

50   Drooping branches tickle my face as I pass

51 underneath the willow. The weather is so warm and dry

52 in Australia that my grandmother rarely uses the drying

53 machine in the laundry house. Instead, Doosie hangs her

54 laundry on a weblike system of rubber-covered ropes

55 wrapped around metal bars. The whole thing resembles

56 an immense umbrella. The sheets flap in the warm

57 breeze and remind me of the sails of yachts gathering in

58 a harbor to start a race. I cross the crunching gravel and

59 enter the cool dimness of Doosie's house. Leaning

60 against the cool brick, I close my eyes and try to ingrain

61 everything in my memory. When I'm at home, the

62 warmth and happiness these memories bring are enough

63 to cheer me up on any occasion.

underneath–under
willow–tree with thin branches that fall to the ground

gathering–meeting

dimness–darkness

ingrain–fix, put in the mind

cheer up–make happy

❓ Why is it important for Sophie to remember her grandmother's place?

Worksheet B

Read the details that Sophie collected about her grandmother's place.

What it looks like	lush, curving driveway, colored plants and trees, stone wall, big gum tree, bright, beautiful, wild, yellow weeds, tennis court
What type of person he/she is	
Where the place is	in a suburb of Sydney, in Australia
What it sounds like	crunch like autumn leaves, grandmother's voice
What it smells like	gardenias smell like honey, hydrangeas smell like apple juice
What it tastes like	
How it moves	
What it feels like	bark scratches, hot breeze, soft ground, intense heat, cool shade, weeds prickle my legs
How it is used or what it does	my mother and her brother used to walk in the garden, my mother used to play on the tennis court, new tenants do not take care of the garden
What kind of person he/she is	
What my subject makes me feel like	warm, secure, happy

For use with Pupil's Edition pp. 412–419

Worksheet C

Fill in the chart with the details about your subject.

What it looks like	
What type of person he/she is	
Where the place is	
What it sounds like	
What it smells like	
What it tastes like	
How it moves	
What it feels like	
How it is used or what it does	
What kind of person he/she is	
What my subject makes me feel like	

Worksheet D

Writing Workshop

Fill in the blanks below to help you start your writing. Use another sheet of paper if you need more space.

Subject of my description:_____

What is special or interesting about the subject:

_____

_____

_____

What I see when I look at my subject

from left to right: _____

from far: _____

from near: _____

from top: _____

from bottom: _____

What I see first: _____

What I see next: _____

What I see last: _____

The most important details about my subject are:

_____

The least important details about my subject are:

_____

How I feel about my subject:

_____

Transition words help link ideas together. They show how ideas are related to one another. The transition words and phrases below help to show position, or the location of something.

in front of	**underneath**	**next to**
behind	**to the left**	**near**
on top of	**to the right**	**under**
in the middle	**above**	**over**
at the bottom	**below**	**around**

For use with Pupil's Edition pp. 412–419

Worksheet E

Writing Workshop

Read over the first draft of your writing and share it with a friend. Then discuss the following questions and write down your answers.

1. What more can I say to identify my subject?

_____

_____

2. What more could I say about why it is special or interesting to me?

_____

_____

_____

3. What details could I add?

_____

_____

_____

_____

4. Are the details arranged in the best way? What details, if any, are out of place?

_____

_____

5. What words or expression could I change to give a clearer picture of my subject?

_____

_____

6. What more could I say at the end of my draft to tell how I feel about my subject?

_____

_____

_____

CHAPTER 19

Focused Description

Background Information

This CD and set of worksheets will take your students through the steps of clearly describing persons, places, or things that are special or interesting to them.

Vocabulary for Description

Refer to pages 7–9 for strategies to use in presenting students with the following words and definitions:

description—something said or written that presents a picture to the person who hears or reads it

focus—to concentrate on something

detail—a piece of information

transition words—words that show how ideas are connected to one another

Guiding Your Writers

See How It's Done

- Before students turn to Worksheet A, you might show them a picture of a house with a lush garden in an encyclopedia or other source. Tell students that they will learn about a special place in the description they are about to read.

- To prepare students for the vocabulary they will encounter on the worksheet, you may want to go over the terms and definitions listed there.

- Have students answer the questions that follow each paragraph on Worksheet A to check their comprehension of the model. After they have completed Worksheet A, see if they are able to describe what the grandmother's place looks like.

- Before students proceed with the workshop, you may wish to read aloud other descriptions of people, places, or things from newspaper articles or stories.

- **Worksheet A Possible answers:**

  ❓ What is Sophie going to write about? her grandmother's house **Why?** The house makes her feel warm and secure.

  ❓ What does she see on her left? a mass of brilliantly colored plants and trees **On her right?** a waist-high stone wall

  ✎ Underline the details that tell about what Sophie smells. honey-sweet gardenias; hydrangeas smell as sweet as freshly pressed apple cider **Circle what she hears.** my grandmother's chattering voice

  ✎ Underline the words that describe how the garden is different now. gnarly bushes; wild beauty; rotting tree stump

  ❓ What is Sophie describing in this paragraph? the old tennis court

  ❓ Why is it important for Sophie to remember her grandmother's place? The happy memories cheer her up.

For use with Pupil's Edition pp. 412–419

Focused Description

Do It Yourself

❶ Prewriting ....

- To help students find ideas, have them do some freewriting. Tell them to start by making a list of all the places and people they know and that they find interesting. Then have them add objects they own that have special meaning to the list. Encourage them to look at photographs, postcards, or read letters they may have received.

- After they have picked their ideas, tell students to close their eyes and think about how their subjects make them feel. Does thinking about their subjects make them feel happy? Invite them to think why that is.

- If a student is having trouble deciding on what to describe, suggest that the student share his or her lists with a partner. The partner can then select one or two ideas that seem the most interesting. Refer to page 4 for strategies to use in grouping students.

- Using the chart on Worksheet B as an example, show students how to complete Worksheet C.

- Have students use any photos or pictures they have brought to class to help them complete the chart. Invite them to picture their subject in their minds and think about sensory details.

- Before students begin filling in the chart on Worksheet C, point out that the subjects they will write about may or may not have characteristics corresponding to all the headings.

❷ Drafting ....

- Allow each student to select an organizational plan that seems most suited to the characteristics of his or her subject. Suggest that spatial order is good for describing things while order of impressions may be better suited for people or places. After students have completed their organized lists, have each read his or her list to a partner. The partner can suggest ways of improving the organizational plan to give a clearer picture of the subject.

- Allow students who have a great deal of difficulty with English to skip filling in the last part of Worksheet D.

- After students complete Worksheet D, discuss with them what they wrote. At this time, suggest to each student the option of the following three that you feel best suits the student's level of language proficiency:

Option 1
Ask the student to look over his or her work on Worksheet D to be sure that details have been chosen carefully and that complete sentences have been written. After making changes to improve the work, the student should hand in the worksheet to you.

Option 2
Ask the student to write a single paragraph in which he or she identifies an object, tells what makes it special or interesting, and describes it. Tell the student to include as many details in the description as possible.

Focused Description

Option 3

Ask the student to write a description that includes three or more paragraphs. Suggest the following structure:

Introduction (one paragraph)
Write a paragraph that tells what you will be describing and what is special or interesting about it.

Body (one or more paragraphs)
Write one or more paragraphs that describe the subject. Include as many details as you can in your description.

Conclusion (one paragraph)
Write a paragraph that tells how you feel about your subject.

- Before students begin writing, suggest that they turn to you or to other students for any help they might need in choosing the right words to describe their subjects.

- As students begin writing their drafts, encourage them to refer to the transition words and phrases listed at the bottom of Worksheet D.

❸ Revising

- Refer to page 4 for some useful strategies for setting up peer-reader pairs.

- Emphasize to students that they can make as many changes as they like until they are happy with their writing.

❹ Editing and Proofreading

- Refer to pages 12–13 for help in presenting students with strategies for proofreading their work.

❺ Sharing and Reflecting

- The questions for reflection will help prepare students for writing their next description. Have students discuss their answers with you.

- Encourage students to share their writing. Suggest that students read their papers to themselves twice before reading them aloud so as to be familiar with the text. Remind students to follow punctuation marks and pause after periods.

- If students are maintaining writing portfolios, you may wish to have them include their worksheets and finished papers to their portfolios for future reference.

- Encourage students to try writing stories that include descriptions. Tell students to follow the steps they used in completing this workshop.

For use with Pupil's Edition pp. 412–419

Interpretive Essay

Writing Workshop

When you hear a tone (TONE), pause the CD and follow the instructions. Pause the CD at any time you don't understand something. You might also ask your teacher or another student for help.

See How It's Done

When you and your friends hear a new song, you probably talk about what it means and how it makes you feel. Perhaps you wonder about one of the lines, or you may think the ending is really talking about you. When you think about what a piece of literature means, you are doing the same thing you did with the song. When you write about literature, you are writing an **interpretation.**

◆ Turn to Worksheet A. Listen to the first paragraph that a student wrote about a story. Then, read the rest of Worksheet A on your own. Read the questions and discuss the answers with a friend. (TONE)

Do It Yourself

Think about poems or stories you have read that had interesting or puzzling meanings. Pick a story or poem that interests you and write about what you think it means.

❶ Prewriting ....

Choose a poem or story to write about.

1. Make a list of the stories and poems you have read on your own or in school this year. Choose one you want to examine.

2. Here are several stories and poems you might want to write about:

   "Afro-American Fragment" by Langston Hughes

   "Birches" by Robert Frost

   "Poem at Thirty-Nine" by Alice Walker

3. Ask your teacher or librarian to help you find a story or poem that interests you.

   ◆ Pause the CD and look for a poem or story to write about. (TONE)

Write some notes about the story or poem you chose.

After you have chosen a piece of literature, read it again and write for five or ten minutes about what you think the piece is about. Do not worry about writing in full sentences; just try to write what happens in the piece and what you think. Then, read the piece again and write down any details that confuse you. Rate your understanding on a scale of 0 to 10 after each reading. Worksheet B will help you do this.

   ◆ Fill out Worksheet B. You can use the back of the page to do your freewriting. Then talk to your teacher about your ideas. (TONE)

Pick a main idea to write about.

Read over the notes you wrote on Worksheet B and think about all your ideas. Which idea do you want to write about? Here are two ideas:

1. Explain why you think a character or characters did something. For example, Adam thinks the survivors started a new way of life because humans are very strong.

CHAPTER 20

Interpretive Essay

2. Explain the author's message. In his paper, Adam explains what Benét thinks about modern technology.

◆ Pause the CD and pick a main idea to write about. Write your idea on Worksheet C. (TONE)

❷ Drafting ....

Organize your ideas.

1. The first part is the introduction. A good way to introduce, or start, your paper is to give the title of the story or poem and then briefly tell what it is about.

2. The second part is the main part, or body, of the paper. In this part, give your thesis statement or main idea. Then, explain your idea. Give examples and details from the short story or poem to support your main idea. A good way to support your idea is to use quotations from the story. See how Adam did this in lines 38–39.

3. The last part is the conclusion. In it, you say your main idea again in a different way. See how Adam does this in lines 56–62.

◆ Fill out Worksheet C to help you organize your writing. (TONE)

Begin writing a draft of your paper.

Use what you wrote on Worksheet C to help you. Look at the student model on Worksheet A. Notice how Adam uses lines from the story as part of his paper (see lines 38 and 39). Look on page 424 of your textbook if you need help with using quotation marks around lines you take directly from the poem or story.

◆ Before you begin writing, talk with your teacher about how you will present your ideas and what your finished writing will look like. (TONE)

❸ Revising ....

Read over what you have written.

Ask a friend to read it too. Then talk about how you can make your paper better. One way to make your writing better is by varying your sentences. Notice how Adam uses a question in lines 15-17 and shorter sentences in lines 32–33. If you need help varying your sentences, you may ask your teacher or a classmate. You might also look on page 27 of this book for practice with combining short sentences.

◆ Turn to Worksheet D. Discuss the questions about your writing with your friend. Then write the answers. (TONE)

❹ Editing and Proofreading ....

Change your writing until you are happy with it.

Think about the answers to the questions on Worksheet D. You could also ask your teacher to suggest changes.

◆ Now make changes in your paper. (TONE)

For use with Pupil's Edition pp. 420–427

Interpretive Essay

Writing Workshop

Proofread your paper.

After you have finished changing your paper, proofread it to find mistakes. Then, make a clean, final copy of your paper.

◆ Ask your teacher how to proofread your writing for mistakes. Then share your writing with others. (TONE)

❺ Sharing and Reflecting ....

Think about what you have learned.

What did you learn as you did this writing? What special problems did you have when you wrote? What would you do differently next time?

◆ Think about these questions and be ready to discuss your answers with your teacher and your classmates. (TONE)

CHAPTER 20

Worksheet A

Here is a literary interpretation that a student, Adam Moses, wrote. As you read, think about why Adam chose this story to write about. The underlined words and phrases may be unfamiliar to you. They are explained on the right side of the page. Circle any other words you don't understand and ask your teacher for help.

CHAPTER 20

"By the Waters of Babylon"
by Adam Moses

1   Stephen Vincent Benét's "By the Waters of Babylon"

2 could easily be interpreted as a <u>doomsday</u> <u>forecast</u>.

3 Obviously, Benét feels that technology is putting the

4 world on the track to <u>Armageddon</u>. However, Benét

5 believes in humankind's <u>resilience</u> and its ability to look

6 toward the future even when that future looks <u>bleak</u>.

7   Before the point at which the story begins, the

8 majority of humanity has been destroyed during a war

9 <u>waged</u> with advanced technologies. In the story, John, the

10 main character, visits the site of a destroyed city and

11 realizes not only the enormous loss brought about by the

12 war but also the danger everywhere in trying to have too

13 much too fast.

14   Benét makes it clear that the technologies were to

15 blame for the catastrophe, but is it correct to say that

16 Benét has a completely dark view of <u>human nature</u>

17 simply because of these technologies? The only reason

18 that humans had these weapons in the first place was

19 their constant <u>quest</u> for more knowledge, which was

20 followed by the development of more technology. Benét

21 is not <u>cursing</u> humans for inventing such weapons; he is

22 <u>merely</u> saying that people sometimes move too quickly in

doomsday–the end of the world
forecast–guessing in advance what will happen
Armageddon–big final war

resilience–strength
bleak–hopeless

❓ What literary work is Adam writing about? Underline his thesis statement. (TONE)

waged–made against

❓ What is Adam telling in this paragraph?

human nature–the way humans are

quest–search, hunt

cursing–wishing bad things to
merely–only

     For use with Pupil's Edition pp. 420–427

Worksheet A (cont.)   *Writing Workshop*

23 | their quest for more knowledge. In the search for more

24 | knowledge, humans discovered how to develop weapons

25 | of immense power. Much knowledge brings positive

26 | consequences; but some new information permits

27 | destruction, such as in the development of weapons.

> ✏ **Underline what Adam thinks is the main idea of the author.**

28 | However, Benét finds plenty of reasons to <u>praise</u>

praise–say good things about

29 | humankind. For example, the <u>very fact</u> that anyone was

very fact–same fact

30 | capable of surviving the <u>Great Burning</u> is a hopeful sign.

Great Burning–a major event talked about in the story

31 | But more important is that societies were able to form

32 | again after the war took place. There was a horrible war.

33 | Millions <u>upon</u> millions were killed. Yet, resilient species

upon–on, after

34 | that we are, humankind was able to come back and start a

35 | society going again. Essentially, the worst thing that

36 | could possibly happen to us happens in this story–the

37 | Great Burning. But how do the <u>survivors</u> react? By

survivors–people who did not die

38 | starting <u>right</u> back up again! Their "women <u>spin wool</u> on

right–immediately
spin wool–make wool

39 | the wheel," and their "priests wear a white robe," just like

40 | in the day before the Great Burning. Progress is in effect,

41 | and everything can grow again.

> ✏ **Underline phrases Adam took from the story. How can you tell?**

42 | An additional positive aspect of human nature, Benét

43 | <u>stresses</u>, is our ability to learn from our mistakes. John's

stresses–makes important

44 | father advises him against telling the people that the

45 | <u>residents</u> of the Place of the Gods were actually humans.

residents–people who live in that place

46 | John agrees, for he knows what happened in the old days

47 | when they "ate knowledge too fast"–there was a Great

48 | Burning. If his people were to eat too much knowledge,

49 | who knows what might happen? And since one cannot be

CHAPTER 20

50 | sure of what might happen, why <u>risk</u> it? Too much

51 | knowledge too fast can lead to very bad things. John

52 | and his father have learned this from the past and they

risk–take a chance

53 | don't make the same mistake. People can learn from

54 | the past and make the appropriate <u>adjustments</u> in their

adjustments–changes

55 | own lives.

? What is the main idea of this paragraph?

56 | Benét doesn't care much for the technology that

57 | results in loss of many lives. But otherwise, he has a

58 | <u>favorable</u> opinion of humankind. "By the Waters of

favorable–good

59 | Babylon" is not just a <u>prediction</u> of <u>world-wide</u>

prediction–guess of what will happen in the future

world-wide–all over the world

60 | destruction but a belief that humanity will learn from

61 | mistakes and <u>recover</u> a civilization lost by unwise

recover–return to, find again

62 | choices.

? What is Adam's conclusion about the main idea of the story?

For use with Pupil's Edition pp. 420–427

Worksheet B

Writing Workshop

Think about your story or poem as you fill out this worksheet.

Title: _____ Author: _____

What I think this piece of literature is about: _____

_____

_____

_____

_____

_____

_____

My understanding of this piece of literature from 0 (poor) to 10 (very good): _____

Parts of the poem or story that puzzle me	My ideas and questions about these parts
1.	
2.	
3.	
4.	

After my second reading, I rate my understanding of this piece of literature from 0 (poor) to 10 (very good): _____

Worksheet C

Fill out this worksheet to help you organize your writing. Use the notes you wrote on Worksheet B to help you.

Start your paper by naming the title and author of the poem or story.

Title _____ Author _____

Next, say what the poem or story is about:

_____

_____

_____

_____

State your main idea about the poem or story:

_____

_____

_____

Give details to help explain the main idea:

_____

_____

_____

Give more details that explain the main idea:

_____

_____

_____

End the paper by repeating the main idea:

_____

_____

_____

Worksheet D

Writing Workshop

Read over the first draft of your writing. Share it with a friend and answer the following questions together. Then write down the answers.

1. Did I name the literary work and tell my readers enough about it? If not, how can I change the first part of my paper?

_____

_____

_____

2. How could I state my main idea more clearly?

_____

_____

_____

3. What details could I add to make my paper clearer and more interesting?

_____

_____

_____

_____

4. Did I use different types of sentences? Which ones could I change to vary my sentences?

_____

_____

_____

5. Is there anything more I could say about what the poem or story means?

_____

_____

_____

_____

CHAPTER 20

Interpretive Essay

Background Information

This material directs students to write an interpretation of a piece of literature by stating a main idea and supporting it with details from the piece. It also helps them write about their reactions to a piece of literature.

Vocabulary for Writing an Interpretive Essay

Before students begin this Workshop, review the following words with them. For various strategies on presenting vocabulary to students acquiring English, turn to pages 7–9.

interpretation—explaining the meaning of something

quotation—repeating a passage or a word from a piece of literature

essay—a short piece of writing that tells about a subject from the writer's personal point of view

main idea—the most important idea

support—details and examples from the literary work that help explain an idea about it

Guiding Your Writers

See How It's Done

- Before students listen to the CD, hold a class discussion about the meaning of song lyrics or a movie in which there is a question about what something means. After students give their ideas about the meaning of the lyrics or movie, tell them that they can also think about the meaning of a story or poem in the same way.

- Before students read the student paper on Worksheet A, you might wish to review the vocabulary words listed on the Worksheet.

- Review the questions and discuss the answers on Worksheet A with your students.

   ❓ **What literary work is Adam writing about?** "By the Waters of Babylon" **Underline his thesis statement.** However, Benét believes in humankind's resilience and its ability to look toward the future even when that future looks bleak.

   ❓ **What is Adam telling in this paragraph?** the plot; what happened

   ✎ **Underline what Adam thinks is the main idea of the author.** Much knowledge brings positive consequences; but some new information permits the destruction, such as in the development of weapons.

   ✎ **Underline phrases Adam took from the story.** women spin wool on the wheel; priests wear a white robe **How can you tell?** They are surrounded by quotation marks.

For use with Pupil's Edition pp. 420–427

Interpretive Essay

❓ What is the main idea of this paragraph? People can learn from their mistakes.

❓ What is Adam's conclusion about the main idea of the story? It's about destruction. It's also about people learning from their mistakes.

Do It Yourself

❶ Prewriting ....

- When students pause the CD and begin looking for a poem or story to write about, here are some ways you can help them:

- Your school librarian may be able to help you locate poems or stories with topics and vocabulary levels that will appeal to student acquiring English.

- Encourage your students to talk with one another about stories that they especially like and want to recommend.

- Explain to students that they may use the back of Worksheet B if necessary.

- When students have completed Worksheet B, put them into small groups and have them share their ideas with one another. They may even read parts of their poems or stories to one another quietly and discuss the meanings of parts they find difficult.

- If students are having trouble finding a main idea, you might suggest that they try one of the following:

  ✓ Circle the item in column 1 on Worksheet B that is the most interesting to them and make a cluster to develop more ideas.

  ✓ Think about what the title of their piece means.

  ✓ Freewrite about the most puzzling part of the piece of literature.

❷ Drafting ....

- Have students show you their completed Worksheets C. Go over their main ideas and help them choose details from the literary work that support those ideas. Use examples from the student paper on Worksheet A to help them understand the use of details.

- You may wish to encourage some of your students to quote lines from their poem or story. Give them some examples of ways to use quotation marks correctly.

- Depending on the English proficiency of your students, you may wish to give them one of the following options for their papers:

CHAPTER 20

Interpretive Essay

Option 1

The student writes a one-paragraph paper that identifies a literary work and author and explains the overall meaning of the work.

Option 2

The student writes a paper of three paragraphs that identifies a piece of literature, explains what it is about, and uses details to discuss the meaning.

Option 3

The student writes a longer paper that identifies the literary work, explains what it is about, interprets one or two key elements, and uses quotations as part of the supporting details.

❸ Revising

- As students begin Worksheet D, remind them that the responses of a peer reader can help them find the parts of their paper that may be confusing or may need more details. The details they use when they answer their peer readers' questions are probably the details they need to add to their paper. For help in choosing peer readers and in establishing a supportive classroom atmosphere, see pages 4–6.

❹ Editing and Proofreading

- When students are ready to make their final copies, meet with them individually and explain the proofreading process you want them to follow. Depending on each student's English proficiency, you may choose to emphasize specific types of errors. See pages 12–13 for various ways to approach proofreading with your students.

❺ Sharing and Reflecting

- As students add this paper to their writing folders or portfolios, have them reflect on their writing by thinking about what they discovered as they worked on this assignment. What would they do differently another time?

- Provide suggestions on sharing their writing through different modes of communication. Students may share their essays orally or in print, or they may be more comfortable sharing through visual aides or electronic means.

- Review the skills students used in writing an interpretation. These skills will help students interpret what they hear in the media, write about the meaning of historical events, or consider the meaning of a piece of art.

For use with Pupil's Edition pp. 420–427

CHAPTER 20

Cause-and-Effect Essay

Writing Workshop

When you hear a tone (TONE), pause the CD and follow the instructions. Pause the CD any time you don't understand something. You might also ask your teacher or classmates for help.

See How It's Done

Why did you win the race? Why did the president write a law to protect animals? Writing about why and how things happen is a good way to learn and to share what you know.

◆ Listen to the first paragraph and question of the model on Worksheet A. Then, pause the CD and read the rest of Worksheet A on your own. Discuss the model and the questions with your teacher. (TONE)

Do It Yourself

For this assignment you will write about why and how something happened. You will write about the **causes,** or reasons for, and event, as well as the **effects.** Effects are the results of an event.

❶ Prewriting ....

Begin exploring ideas to write about.

Here are two ways to get started:

1. Make a list of things you have done and are proud of. It could be winning a race, passing an exam, getting a job, or getting in better shape. Next to each thing, write why it happened.

2. Look through newspapers and magazines to find events or ideas that you'd like to understand better. Make a list of those topics.

◆ Now pause the CD and make your lists. (TONE)

Choose a topic for your paper.

Look at the ideas you have written. Which idea interests you the most? Which idea do you know the most about? You might want to ask several friends which idea they would prefer to read about.

◆ Pause the CD and choose a topic. Discuss it with your teacher. (TONE)

Think about your topic.

Remember these facts about causes and effects as you think about your topic: A cause is the reason something happens. An effect is what happens because of the cause. One cause can have more than one effect.

Then, think about your topic. What is its cause? What are its effects? Are the effects the results of the cause you named?

Next, think about your audience, or readers. Who will read your paper? What do your readers already know about your topic? Think about the information you will need to give to your readers.

◆ Now answer the questions on Worksheet B. (TONE)

Cause-and-Effect Essay

Writing Workshop

Find more information about your topic.

You need to learn more about why and how the event happened. You can brainstorm ideas with a friend. You can also ask your teacher or school librarian to help you do research at a library. Write down all the facts, quotations, and details that will help explain the cause and effects of your topic.

♦ Pause the CD and find more information about your topic. (TONE)

❷ Drafting ....

Organize the information you have collected.

You need to clearly identify the cause and effects of your topic. A cause-and-effect chart can help you do this. Fill in the chart on Worksheet C with information about your topic. Write the effects in the order they happened. Then add details to answer questions such as how, why, when, and who.

♦ Now turn to Worksheet C and fill in the chart with information about your topic. (TONE)

Start drafting your cause-and-effect essay.

You have already begun your writing on Worksheets B and C. Now you will turn your information into an essay. Follow these hints to help you organize your work:

1. An easy way to organize a cause-and effect essay is to describe one cause, and then explain its many effects. For example, in his paper, Jason explains how joining the track club led him to run cross-country, to win gold medals, and to win the state finals.

2. Start by writing the cause and effect of your topic. Next, give background information. See how Jason Nemo does this in the second paragraph of his essay (lines 10–19). Then, write the different effects of the cause you wrote at the beginning. End by summarizing the cause and its effects in one or two sentences. Look at Jason's ending in lines 60–64 of his paper.

3. Make sure to write the effects in chronological order, that is, in the order in which they happened.

♦ Pause the CD. Talk with your teacher about how your final paper will look. Then begin your draft. (TONE)

❸ Revising ....

Read over what you have written.

Ask a friend to read it too. You might want to ask your friend to explain the cause and its effects to you in his or her own words.

♦ Now turn to Worksheet D. With your friend, discuss the questions about your writing. Then write down the answers. (TONE)

❹ Editing and Proofreading ....

Decide how to make your writing better.

Think about your answers to the questions on Worksheet D. You could also ask your friend or teacher to suggest changes.

♦ Now begin changing your writing. (TONE)

For use with Pupil's Edition pp. 428–435

Cause-and-Effect Essay

Writing Workshop

Continue changing your writing until you are happy with it.
You may want to ask your teacher for help on how to proofread your paper for
mistakes. Pay special attention to the verbs. Do they all agree with their subjects?
For help with subject-verb agreement, see page 432 of your book.

◆ Make a final clean copy of your cause-and-effect essay. (TONE)

❺ Sharing and Reflecting ....

Think about what you have learned by writing a cause-and-effect essay.
Share your final copy with an audience. You may want to record your essay and
play it for your classmates. You may also copy it and publish it in the school paper.

Think about what you learned while writing the essay. How did you solve any
problems that you had? How was this type of writing different from other writing
you have done? What have you learned about the cause and effect relationship?

◆ Think about these questions and be ready to discuss your answers with your teacher and
your classmates. (TONE)

CHAPTER 2t

Worksheet A

This is an essay that one student wrote about an important sports event. As you read his paper, think about the effects he writes. Words that you may find difficult to understand are underlined and are explained on the right side of the page. Circle any other words that you don't understand, and ask your teacher for help.

Moments
by Jason Nemo

1   I've just run in the state championship 3200-meter

2 relay race with three teammates. We won! In the past I

3 usually chalked up our wins to raw talent, but winning

4 this event in a state meet made me realize how far from

5 raw my talent is. I had actually started working out in

6 seventh or eighth grade. The training that began back

7 then made this victory possible. After the race, I jogged

8 around the track to cool off, and I reflected on the stages

9 of training that led me to this moment.

10   The summer before I entered high school I joined a

11 track club, where I was able to compete against other

12 clubs for the first time. Our team was good enough to

13 participate in a national meet, so we were able to

14 practice our skills against other track clubs from all over

15 the country. We were often pitted against imposing relay

16 teams of 12-and 13-year olds who looked like cousins of

17 the Incredible Hulk. Even though we were just training

18 for the upcoming school year, I felt more inadequate

19 than I have ever felt in my running career. The effect of

20 those competitions was that I learned to overcome

21 whatever doubts I had about myself and just run as well

22 as I knew I could.

relay–running in teams

chalked up–thought it was because
raw–natural
meet–race
working out–exercising

training–practice

jogged–ran slowly

❓ What does Jason say is the cause of his victory? (TONE)

track–running

pitted–made to compete
imposing–to be admired, scary

Incredible Hulk–comic book super hero
upcoming–next
inadequate–not good enough

✏️ Circle one main cause. Then underline one of its effects.

For use with Pupil's Edition pp. 428–435

23	That fall I ran <u>cross-country</u> for my school. If	*cross-country*–on roads and paths
24	running two or three miles in a cross-country meet across	
25	<u>rugged terrain</u> in pouring rain doesn't build your	*rugged terrain*–bumpy ground
26	<u>stamina</u>, I don't know what will. Daily practices	*stamina*–energy, strength
27	throughout the fall and spring paid off when I was named	
28	best freshman in the <u>conference</u> in the 400-meter event.	*conference*–group
29	It was the first time I had <u>distinguished</u> myself in my	*distinguished*–done something noticeable
30	sport. <u>Consequently</u>, my pride and <u>confidence</u> increased,	*Consequently*–Because of that
31	and I was ready to push myself to the next level.	**? What are two effects of Jason's practice?**
32	The following summer, I practiced every morning	
33	for the fall cross-country season. By <u>steamy</u> August we	*confidence*–knowing that you can do something
34	were pushing six to eight miles a day. It was hard work,	*steamy*–hot and humid
35	but all that cross-country running had prepared me for it.	
36	The <u>highlight</u> of my career came in the last meet of the	*highlight*–best part
37	season, on our <u>archrival's</u> track. I won all three races,	*archrival*–main enemy
38	including the 400-meter, which I won with my fastest	
39	time ever. I left the track with three gold medals. As a	
40	result, I knew that <u>expectations</u> would be high for next	*expectations*–hopes, goals
41	year. That was fine with me. My expectations for myself	
42	had been increasing with each new success.	**? What did Jason do in August? What did he do next?**
43	Because of all our success, everyone <u>was expecting</u>	
44	us to go all the way. Our hard work and training paid off	*was expecting*–thought we would
45	and we made it to the big show—the state finals. I was a	
46	<u>wreck</u> before the race. I had been nervous about races	*wreck*–very nervous
47	before, though, so I knew that I could <u>overcome</u> it. I	*overcome*–get over
48	stepped onto that big blue track, looking into the huge	
49	crowd with my whole season on the line. If I could excel	

CHAPTER 21

Worksheet A (cont.)

Writing Workshop

50 | at all the meets before now, I told myself, I could do the

51 | same here at the state championship.

> **?** **What was the effect of the team's hard work?**

52 | My legs felt like <u>lead</u>. When the gun went off the

lead–heavy metal

53 | <u>jitters</u> wouldn't go away, and I hardly noticed the race. I

jitters–nervous, shaking

54 | finished my <u>leg</u> of the race in less than two minutes,

leg—part

55 | which was a record run for me. Even in my nervous state,

56 | I had <u>exceeded</u> my expectations for myself. A couple of

exceeded–done better than

57 | minutes later my teammate crossed the finish line. I

58 | looked up and saw that we had won. Still <u>exhausted</u>, I

exhausted–very tired

59 | <u>hobbled</u> over to my teammates to share the victory.

> **?** **What did Jason and his team do?**

60 | Thanks to four years of training, facing intimidating

hobbled–walked weakly

61 | opponents, and proving my abilities to myself and others,

62 | my team and I had proven ourselves winners. With sweat

63 | still pouring off my face, I was already thinking about

64 | next year's team.

> **?** **What was the cause of the event Jason wrote about? What was its effect?**

For use with Pupil's Edition pp. 428–435

Worksheet B

Writing Workshop

Write down your topic, then answer the questions about it.

The event I am going to write about is

_____

What caused this to happen?

_____

_____

_____

What happened because of it?

_____

_____

What details do I know about the cause and effects of my topic?

_____

_____

_____

What do I need to learn?

_____

_____

Where can I find the information I need?

_____

_____

_____

_____

CHAPTER 21

Worksheet C

Fill in the chart below with information about your topic. Make sure to write the effects in the order they happened. Use your own paper if you need more space or need to add boxes to the chart.

Topic:

Effect 1:

Details:

Cause:

Details:

Effect 2:

Details:

Effect 3:

Details:

CHAPTER 21

For use with Pupil's Edition pp. 428–435

Worksheet D

Writing Workshop

Read over the first draft of your writing and share it with a friend. Answer the following questions together. Then write down the answers.

1. Did I clearly write a cause and effect in the beginning? How could I explain it more clearly?

_____

_____

_____

2. How could I make my introduction more interesting?

_____

_____

_____

3. What other details could I add to explain the cause and effects more clearly?

_____

_____

_____

4. Did I write the effects in time order? Is any effect in the wrong place? If so, where should it be in the essay?

_____

_____

_____

5. How could I make the connections between the cause and the effects clearer?

_____

_____

_____

6. What other important effects could I add?

_____

_____

_____

CHAPTER 21

Cause-and-Effect Essay

Background Information

To make this Writing Workshop more accessible to students acquiring English, the search for topics has been narrowed. Also only one organizational scheme, describing one cause leading to many effects, has been presented. You might want to discuss other schemes with students whose topics demand them.

Vocabulary for Cause-and-Effect Essay

Before students begin this workshop, make sure that they understand the following related vocabulary. Refer to pages 7–9 for strategies to use in presenting vocabulary.

cause—a reason something happens

effect—something that happens because of something else

connection—a link between two or more thingsafter reading a poem or story

Guiding Your Writers

See How It's Done

- To make sure that students understand cause-and-effect relationships, you might want to do the following activity. Divide the chalkboard in half vertically and label the left side "Event A" and the right side "Event B." Then list several pairs of events in which event B happens because of event A—for example, you plant a seed, water it, and the seed germinates and grows; or you press the brake pedal on a car and the car stops. You might also want to mention a pair of events that are not linked as cause to effect—for example, a car stops and a traffic signal turns red. Then ask students to give other examples of cause-and-effect relationships, and write them on the chalkboard.

- Tell students that a good way to determine if two events are related as cause and effect is to substitute the events in the following sentence: "Because (Event A), therefore (Event B)." If the resulting statement is true, the events are linked as cause and effect.

- After students read the model "Moments" on Worksheet A, ask them to summarize the essay and review the answers to the questions inserted between paragraphs.

- **Worksheet A Possible answers:**

  ❓ **What does Jason say is the cause of his victory?** training

  ✎ **Circle one main cause.** I joined a track club where I was able to compete against other clubs. **Then underline one of its effects.** I learned to overcome whatever doubts I had about myself.

  ❓ **What are two effects of Jason's practice?** He was named best freshman. His pride and confidence increased.

  ❓ **What did Jason do in August?** ran 6 to 8 miles a day; practiced every morning **What did he do next?** He won three gold medals.

CHAPTER 21

For use with Pupil's Edition pp. 428–435

Cause-and-Effect Essay

Teacher's Notes

❓ What was the effect of the team's hard work? They made it to the state finals.

❓ What did Jason and team his do? They won the race.

❓ What was the cause of the event Jason wrote about? four years of training; facing intimidating opponents **What was its effect?** He and his team won an important race.

- Go over the vocabulary items listed on Worksheet A. You can then read the excerpt aloud or ask students to read it silently.

Do It Yourself

❶ Prewriting ....

- To help students find writing ideas, ask them to think about times when they felt they had achieved something.

- Some students might be reluctant to talk about themselves. Encourage them to think about current or past events that interest them and look for their causes and effects.

- When students come to you to discuss their topics, make sure that they have chosen to write about true cause-and-effect relationships. Since most such relationships involve more than one cause or more than one effect, you might want to help students focus their topics to deal with causes that have multiple effects.

- Help students plan their strategies for collecting information about their topics. Remind them that thinking beforehand about exactly what they need to know can help them gather information efficiently, whatever approach they use.

❷ Drafting ....

- You might want to modify the organizational scheme suggested on the CD to suit individual students' topics. For example, if a student is describing an effect that has multiple causes, suggest that he or she first describe the effect and then explain each of the causes.

- Depending on students' individual levels of English proficiency, you may wish to suggest one of the following formats for each student's writing:

Option 1
The student completes Worksheets B and C.

Option 2
The student writes two paragraphs, one describing one cause and the other describing the corresponding effect or effects.

Option 3
The student writes a paper of more than three paragraphs, in which he or she identifies a cause, describes the situation, gives several effects, uses examples and quotations, and concludes by showing how the cause and effects were important to him or her.

Cause-and-Effect Essay

❸ Revising ....

- Remind students that the most important goal of their writing is to explain the connection between effects and causes clearly.

- See page 4 for suggestions on pairing students for peer-response activities. Remind students that they should feel free to ask either you or their peer readers for specific suggestions on improving their writing.

❹ Editing and Proofreading ....

- When students are ready to make their final drafts, meet with them individually and explain the proofreading process you'd like them to use. Your expectations may be determined by each student's English proficiency. Various approaches to proofreading are detailed on pages 12–13.

- Students may benefit from reviewing subject-verb agreement before they check their papers. Invite them to identify each verb's subject and check the agreement.

❺ Sharing and Reflecting ....

- Ask students to think seriously about their writing process and final product. You might also ask them to consider what they have learned about how they think and write. Ask them to write out their answers to some or all of these questions.

- Review the skills students used in explaining causes and effects and suggest how these skills might be applicable to other types of writing and in other curricular areas. The ability to recognize and explain causes and effects, in fact, is an essential critical thinking skill that students will use in almost every academic and nonacademic pursuit.

- Have students place their cause-and-effect essays in their Working Portfolios.

- Students may compile their essays in a class newsletter.

For use with Pupil's Edition pp. 428–435

Persuasive Essay

Each time you hear a tone (TONE), pause the CD and follow the instructions. Then restart the CD. Whenever you don't understand something, pause the CD and ask your teacher or a classmate to help you.

See How It's Done

Some colleges want to make it a rule that all their students must own computers. Do you think that this rule is a good idea? You and your friends may not agree about this question. A question or idea that people may not agree about is called an **issue.** When you write what you think about an issue, you are writing your opinion.

◆ Turn to Worksheet A. Listen to the first paragraph of one student's opinion about an issue that is important to him. Read the rest on your own. As you read, answer the questions. Talk about the essay with your teacher and classmates. (TONE)

Do It Yourself

Write your opinion about an issue that is important to you. Try to **persuade** your readers—that is, try to get them to agree with you.

❶ Prewriting ....

Find an issue to write about.

Here are two ways to find ideas:

1. Work with three or four classmates. Together, brainstorm a list of important issues. For example, you may think of school or community problems that need to be solved. You might also think of rules, laws, and customs that seem unfair. You might try to complete a sentence such as: This school would be a better place if _____.

2. Read the newspaper. Look for issues that interest you. Make a list of issues that you could write about.

◆ Make your lists now. Then, read your list and choose an issue that you would like to write about. Tell your teacher which issue you have chosen. (TONE)

Think about your issue and your opinion.

Talk with classmates about your issue. Ask your classmates what they think about the issue. Together, talk about why your issue is important. Try to understand both sides of your issue—the two ways of looking at it. Then make notes about your issue. Decide what you think about it—what your opinion is. Tell why you think your opinion is right. Look at the other side of the issue, too. Write reasons why some people may not agree with your opinion.

◆ Turn to Worksheet B and use the chart to make notes about your issue. When you finish Worksheet B, show it to your teacher. (TONE)

Think about your readers.

How can you persuade your readers to agree with you? You must understand your readers, and you must help them to understand your opinion. Try to answer these two questions as you think about your readers:

1. Who are my readers?

2. What do my readers need to know about my issue?

Persuasive Essay

Suppose that you believe that college students should own computers. If your readers are your grandparents' age, you would need to explain how computers help with writing and with storing information. However, if your readers are people your own age, they already know how computers can help students. To persuade readers your own age, you might explain how students can get low-cost computers.

◆ With a partner, discuss the two questions about your readers. Plan how to persuade them about your issue. (TONE)

Learn more about your issue.

Write what you already know about the issue. Then, read about your issue in books, magazines, and newspapers. Talk with people who know a lot about it. Take notes. Here are three ways to show your readers why they should agree with you:

1. Find facts or statements that you can prove. When you prove something, you show that it is true. See lines 19–23 of Worksheet A.

2. Find examples that support, or back up, your ideas. Misha does this on lines 39–41.

3. Find out about the ideas of experts—people who know a lot about your issue.

◆ Pause the CD and write ideas about your issue now. Save your notes. (TONE)

❷ Drafting ....

Plan your writing.

Look at all the notes you have taken about your issue. Use Worksheet C to help you make a plan with these four parts:

1. Start by writing a thesis statement. Tell what your issue is and what you think about it. Misha does this by writing, "I believe that this policy doesn't make any sense. Instead, the [Montgomery County Public Schools] should exempt student-athletes from taking P.E. classes" (lines 8–11).

2. State your reasons and support them. Notice how Misha does this in paragraphs 2, 3, and 4.

3. Write about the other side of your issue. Write reasons why readers might disagree with your opinion. Then write an answer to those reasons. Misha does this in the fifth paragraph of his essay.

4. To end, state your opinion once more, in different words. Misha writes, "It is more important for student athletes to become well-rounded academically by taking electives than to take P.E. class since they already understand the value of fitness" (lines 50–53).

◆ Turn to Worksheet C to help you organize your writing. When you finish Worksheet C, show it to your teacher. (TONE)

Write your essay.

Follow the plan you made on Worksheet C. These hints can help you as you write:

1. Be logical when you present your ideas. Make sure your thinking is clear and your ideas flow.

2. Try to avoid ideas that are too general to prove, such as "students love sports."

3. Use facts, statistics, and quotations to support your reasons.

For use with Pupil's Edition pp. 436–445

CHAPTER 22

Persuasive Essay

Writing Workshop

◆ Talk with your teacher about how you will present your information and what your finished writing will look like. Then write your essay. (TONE)

❸ Revising ....

Read your writing and think about it.

When you finish your essay, put it away for a while. Then, read it again and ask a classmate to read it. Are all your opinions backed up with facts?

◆ With your classmate, write answers to the questions on Worksheet D. When you finish, show the worksheet to your teacher. (TONE)

❹ Editing and Proofreading ....

Make a final copy of your writing.

Ask your teacher for help on how to proofread your paper. Make all your changes and a clean copy of your paper.

◆ Make a clean copy now. Then, share it with your classmates. (TONE)

❺ Sharing and Reflecting ....

Think about what you have learned.

Share your persuasive essay by discussing your issue in the form of a debate or speech. You may also wish to change it into a letter to the editor of a local newspaper. Think about your writing. Which part of this writing was hardest for you? How did writing your essay change your ideas?

◆ Think about these questions. Be ready to talk about your answers with your teacher and your classmates. (TONE)

CHAPTER 22

Worksheet A

Below is a paper one student wrote about an issue. Read it and see if you agree with his opinion. Words that you may not understand are underlined and are explained on the right side of the page. Circle any other words that you do not understand, and ask your teacher what they mean.

<u>Extracurricular</u> Sports Should Satisfy State Physical Education Requirement

by Misha Dworsky

1 <u>Track</u>, football, soccer, baseball, basketball, and other	*extracurricular*–after or outside of school
2 sports attract <u>dedicated</u> student athletes who often	*track*–running
3 practice every day after school and then participate in	*dedicated*–willing to give a lot of time
4 weekend games. Should these students be forced to give	
5 up an <u>elective class</u> period to take a required physical	*elective class*–class that is not required
6 education class? In order to meet the state's physical	
7 education (P.E.) course requirements, that is exactly what	
8 Whitman High School asks them to do. I believe that this	
9 <u>policy</u> doesn't make any sense. Instead, the [Montgomery	*policy*–rule, official plan
10 <u>County</u> Public Schools] should <u>exempt</u> student-athletes	*County*–small part of a state *exempt*–excuse
11 from taking P.E. classes.	**❓ What issue is Misha writing about? What is his opinion? (TONE)**
12 First of all, participating in an extracurricular sport	
13 meets the <u>objectives</u> of the state's course requirements.	*objectives*–goals
14 Those objectives are to promote <u>fitness</u> and improve	*fitness*–being healthy
15 athletic skill, according to the Whitman <u>course catalog</u>.	*course catalog*–list of classes
16 Involvement in either a <u>varsity</u> or a club sport for one	*varsity*–team
17 season already makes a student fit and athletically	
18 skilled.	**✏ Underline the first reason for Misha's opinion.**
19 A second reason to change the policy is that the	
20 physical education requirement forces students to give up	
21 an elective class period. High school students can	

For use with Pupil's Edition pp. 436–445

| 22 | generally choose only eight elective courses from <u>dozens</u> | *dozens*–many (dozen=12) |

22 generally choose only eight elective courses from <u>dozens</u>   *dozens*–many (dozen=12)

23 of class offerings. By eliminating the P.E. requirement

24 for student athletes, the county would give students more

25 freedom in selecting their courses. |————————→   **? What is the second reason for his opinion?**

26   Another reason to exempt student athletes is that

27 regular P.E. classes would not be so crowded. A large

28 portion of the student body participates in either varsity

29 or club sports. With smaller classes, teachers could

30 <u>provide</u> more <u>supervision</u> during class periods and be   *provide*–give
supervision–attention

31 more <u>responsive</u> to student <u>feedback</u>. Students in those   *responsive*–willing to pay attention

32 classes would have a greater chance to improve their   *feedback*–opinion

33 athletic skills and confidence. |————————→   **? What is the main idea of this paragraph?**

34   Finally, <u>exposing</u> students to different sports is one   *exposing*–showing

35 goal of the P.E. requirement, but this objective alone is

36 not important enough to require students to take P.E.

37 class. Students <u>seldom</u> take P.E. class as seriously as they   *seldom*–not often

38 would an extracurricular sport, so students do not always

39 appreciate sports they <u>sample</u> in P.E. class. Also, students   *sample*–try

40 have elementary and middle school P.E. classes to try a

41 variety of sports. Most students have already chosen a

42 favorite sport on which to concentrate by the time they

43 reach high school, so it is not <u>worthwhile</u> to make   *worthwhile*–worth the time and effort

44 students spend class time experimenting with different

45 sports. |————————————————→   **✎ Underline the answer Misha gives to people who might disagree with him.**

46   Varsity and club sports require <u>a great deal</u> of time

47 and effort from athletes. The county should recognize   *a great deal*–a lot

48 that team sports encourage physical activity more

CHAPTER 22

Worksheet A (cont.)

Writing Workshop

49	effectively than P.E. class and <u>spark</u> more enthusiasm
50	from students. It is more important for student athletes to
51	become <u>well-rounded</u> academically by taking electives
52	than to take P.E. class, since they already understand the
53	value of fitness.

spark–start

well-rounded–knowing about many different subjects

? **What is Misha's conclusion?**

For use with Pupil's Edition pp. 436–445

CHAPTER 22

Worksheet B

Fill in this chart with notes about both sides of your issue.

The issue:

My opinion:

My reasons:

1.

2.

3.

Reasons to disagree with my opinion:

1.

2.

3.

CHAPTER 22

Worksheet C

Fill in the plan below. After "Support," write facts, examples, and experts' ideas.
Add more reasons to parts 2 and 3 if you wish.

Part 1

Issue: _____

_____

Thesis statement:_____

_____

Part 2

Reason 1: _____

_____

Support: _____

_____

Reason 2: _____

_____

Support: _____

_____

Part 3

Reason to disagree with me: _____

_____

My answer: _____

Reason to disagree with me: _____

_____

My answer: _____

Part 4

How I will end my paper: _____

_____

_____

For use with Pupil's Edition pp. 436–445

CHAPTER 22

Worksheet D

Writing Workshop

With a classmate, write answers to the questions below.

1. How could I make the beginning of my paper more interesting?

_____

_____

2. What other reasons might help me persuade my readers?

_____

_____

3. Where could I add more facts, examples, or experts' ideas to support my opinion?

_____

_____

_____

4. Do I move from one idea to the next in a logical manner? What idea seems out of place and why?

_____

_____

_____

5. What other reasons might people have for disagreeing with me?

_____

_____

_____

6. How could I give better answers to people's reasons for disagreeing with me?

_____

_____

_____

7. How could I make the end of my paper better?

_____

_____

_____

CHAPTER 22

Persuasive Essay

Background Information

This CD and set of worksheets will introduce students to persuasive writing. The assignment focuses on stating an opinion and supporting it with facts.

Vocabulary for Persuasive Essay

You may wish to review some or all of the following terms with your students before beginning this workshop. Refer to pages 7–9 for strategies to use in presenting vocabulary to your students.

issue—a question that people may disagree about

opinion—what a person thinks about an issue

persuade—to get people to agree with you

reasons—statements telling why an opinion seems right

support—to back up an idea or opinion

fact—a statement that can be proved

prove—to show that something is true

expert—someone who knows a lot about an issue

Guiding Your Writers

See How It's Done

- To prepare students to read the model, you might ask them to identify an issue in their school that has caused debate. How does it compare to the issue of student athletes' P.E. requirements described in the model?

- After students have read the model, reinforce their comprehension by asking them to summarize the writer's opinion. Then, to open a discussion, ask whether they agree with the writer. Encourage students to identify the parts of the essay that they found most and least convincing. You might invite them to evaluate the writer's answers to opposing arguments and to suggest other possible answers. As students discuss their opinions of the essay, point out that they are practicing the kind of thinking that they will use in this writing assignment.

- **Worksheet A Possible answers:**

    ❓ **What issue is Misha writing about?** P.E. requirements for student athletes
    What is his opinion? Student athletes should not have to take P.E classes.

    ✏️ **Underline the first reason for Misha's opinion.** participating in extracurricular sports meets the objectives of the state's course requirements.

    ❓ **What is the second reason for his opinion?** Students must give up an elective to take P.E.

    ❓ **What is the main idea of this paragraph?** P.E. classes are too crowded.

For use with Pupil's Edition pp. 436–445

Persuasive Essay

✏️ **Underline the answer Misha gives to people who might disagree with him.** Most students have already chosen a favorite sport on which to concentrate by the time they reach high school, so it is not worthwhile to make students spend class time experimenting with different sports.

❓ **What is Misha's conclusion?** It is more important for student athletes to become well-rounded academically by taking electives than to take P.E. class.

Do It Yourself

❶ Prewriting ....

- Be aware that some students' cultural values may make them uncomfortable with criticizing authority or taking sides in a controversy. Such students might do well with less controversial issues, such as the rescuing of endangered species or the preserving of the environment.

- Students choosing the second option might work in small groups, with each group taking a different section of the newspaper. Thus, students in one group would list international and national issues, while students in other groups would list local issues, issues in sports, health issues, and so on. The groups could then combine their lists.

- You might encourage some students to list issues related to their native lands' histories or traditions.

- Check each student's completed copy of Worksheet B. Make sure the topics they have chosen are narrow enough for their essays. Encourage them to pick topics that are significant to their audience.

- Be sure that you have clearly specified an audience for this assignment. Pair students for discussion and encourage them to help one another speculate about readers' concerns and understanding of the issues.

- You might explain that one way to persuade readers is to work from an idea that both sides agree about.

- You may wish to ask your school's librarian to bring in books and periodicals that students can use to research their issues.

❷ Drafting ....

- Remind students not only to use material from Worksheet B and from their other notes but also to take their readers' needs into account as they complete Worksheet C.

- Check each student's completed copy of Worksheet C.

- Confer individually with students before they begin drafting. You may wish to suggest one of the following three options to each student, depending on his or her level of English proficiency:

CHAPTER 22

Persuasive Essay

Option 1
The student turns in Worksheet C, carefully filled in with complete sentences.

Option 2
In one well-developed paragraph, the student states an opinion; gives reasons for it, supporting at least one reason with at least one fact or example; presents and counters at least one opposing argument; and ends with a summarizing statement.

Option 3
The student writes an essay of three or more paragraphs in which he or she introduces an issue and states an opinion; offers reasons supported by facts, examples, and experts' ideas; presents and counters at least one opposing argument; and concludes with a strong restatement of his or her position.

❸ Revising

- Check each student's completed copy of Worksheet D.

- Confer individually with students before they begin revising. Depending on students' strengths and English proficiency, you may wish to suggest that they focus on only one type of error, such as correcting run-ons as presented in their textbook on page 442. For helpful approaches to proofreading with students acquiring English, see pages 12–13.

❹ Editing and Proofreading

- You might encourage students to exchange their final drafts with the classmates who read their initial drafts and to comment on changes that they notice in their partners' work.

❺ Sharing and Reflecting

- You may wish to have students respond in writing to the questions. Then, to help students reflect on their experiences with this assignment, invite them to share and discuss their responses. You might also ask them to consider the following two questions:

  ✓ How did your classmates help you solve problems with this assignment?

  ✓ If you had more time, how might you change your paper to make it still better?

- Invite students to write their answers to these questions and place them in their Working Portfolios along with their essays.

- You may wish to tell students that the skills used in persuasive writing are helpful in many areas beyond the English classroom. Students who can formulate ideas on the basis of reasoning and research can devise innovative solutions to mathematical problems, create and check scientific hypotheses, and construct sound explanations for historical and social phenomena. Students who can see both sides of an issue gain insights into human behavior, literary works, historical controversies, and current events. Students who can understand others' viewpoints and persuasively state their own can help resolve disagreements and facilitate needed changes.

For use with Pupil's Edition pp. 436–445

Problem-Solution Essay   *Writing Workshop*

When you hear a tone (TONE), pause the CD and follow the instructions. You may also pause the CD at any time and play parts again. If you need more help, ask your teacher or another student.

See How It's Done

What problems do you see in your school, your town, or the world? Does your football team always lose? Is your neighborhood park full of weeds? Does your town run low on water each summer? Writing about problems like these is one way to find good, useful solutions. Writing helps you look more closely at a problem. Then you can think of solutions and decide which ones will work.

◆ Now turn to Worksheet A. Listen to the beginning of a problem-solution essay that one student wrote. Then, continue reading on your own. When you finish, discuss the model and the answers to the questions with your teacher or one of your classmates. (TONE)

Do It Yourself

You will think of a problem, look closely at it, and find solutions. Then you will share your ideas by writing about the problem and its solutions.

❶ Prewriting ....

Find a problem to write about.

Here are two ways to find ideas:

1. Freewrite to find ideas. Write down every problem that you think of. Don't worry whether the problem is a good one or a bad one to write about. While you freewrite, you just want to make a list of ideas. To help you, you may want to write different endings to this sentence: What really bothers me is _____.

2. Ask your friends what problems they think about. Make a list of their ideas.

3. Read your local or school newspaper and list problems that are mentioned.

◆ Pause the CD now and make your lists. (TONE)

Explore different problems.

Look at your lists of problems and choose two or three that interest you. Think about each one for a few minutes. Try to think of some solutions.

◆ Pause the CD and fill in the charts on Worksheet B. (TONE)

Choose a problem to write about.

Pick the problem that interests you the most. It should be a problem that you know a lot about. You should also have an idea of how to solve the problem.

Gather information about the problem you chose.

Talk with friends about the problem and solutions. Take notes of ideas you get from your friends. Decide what you need to know about your problem. You may want to ask your teacher or school librarian for help on how to do research.

CHAPTER 23

Problem-Solution Essay   *Writing Workshop*

Here are ways to find out more information:

1. Talk to an expert. An expert is someone who knows a lot about a subject.
2. Find facts, or statements, that can be shown to be true, to support your solution. Use statistics, or numbers, too.
3. Talk to people who might be helped by your solution.

   ◆ Pause the CD and look for information. Then fill in Worksheet C. It will help you get your ideas about the problem down on paper. (TONE)

❷ Drafting ....

Get ready to write.

Now that you have gathered information about your problem, you are ready to write. Your first step is to organize what you will write. Your essay should have three parts.

1. First, tell what the problem is and why it is important. Another option is to give examples to show what the problem is. That is what Erica Papernik did on Worksheet A. Notice how she illustrates the problem on lines 1–10.
2. In the main part of your essay, you tell why the problem is important. Write down information that supports your ideas. For example, see how Erica uses statistics on line 12. Then, tell what the solution is. Notice how Erica gives a solution to the problem on lines 23–24.
3. End your essay by restating the problem and its solution in different words. You may want to tell how the solution would help the people affected by the problem. Erica does this in lines 31–33.

   ◆ Now pause the CD and complete Worksheet D. It will help you organize your ideas for writing. (TONE)

Begin writing a draft of your paper.

Use what you wrote on Worksheet D to guide your writing. You can add more ideas as you write.

   ◆ Before you begin writing, talk with your teacher about how you will present your ideas and what your finished writing will look like. (TONE)

❸ Revising ....

Think about what you have written.

Then ask a friend to read it too. Read your conclusion. Does it make sense? Does it summarize the problem and its solution clearly?

   ◆ Now turn to Worksheet E. Read and answer the questions with a friend. (TONE)

❹ Editing and Proofreading ....

Change your writing to make it better.

Think about the answers you and your friend gave to the questions on Worksheet E. Decide on changes that will make your writing better. You may want to ask your teacher for help.

   ◆ Now begin changing your writing. (TONE)

CHAPTER 23

For use with Pupil's Edition pp. 446–453

Problem-Solution Essay

Writing Workshop

Continue changing your writing until you are happy with it.

When you are happy with the changes you've made, ask your teacher for instructions about proofreading.

◆ Pause the CD now and make a final copy of your writing. (TONE)

❺ Sharing and Reflecting ....

Think about what you have learned in writing about a problem and its solutions.

What did you learn about your problem and its solutions as you were writing? What special problems did you have while you were writing?

◆ Think about these questions and be ready to discuss your answers with your teacher and your classmates. (TONE)

Share your essay.

You may want to share your essay with people who can solve this problem. Discuss your solution with them. You may want to take notes. Clip the notes to your essay before placing it in your Working Portfolio.

CHAPTER 23

Worksheet A

This is a problem-solution essay that a student wrote. Words and phrases that you may not know are underlined and are explained on the right side of the page. As you read, circle any other words you don't know. Ask your teacher or another student for help with them.

Test Center Needed
by Erica Papernik

1 So you're just getting over being sick, and you have

2 to <u>make up</u> that all-important test. You take out your

3 number-two pencil and start. All of a sudden another

4 student comes in for help, so a teacher starts going over

5 yesterday's lessons. You then try to <u>block</u> that <u>out</u> when

6 another teacher walks in and <u>runs off</u> 100 copies. Then,

7 off in the background, you can hear two teachers <u>gabbing</u>

8 about what they want to eat for lunch. Now you can't

9 concentrate, and you're going to fail the test. This is. . .

10 your life.

11 Many students are being hurt by being forced to take

12 tests in noisy rooms. Last semester, over 3,149 students

13 had to make up tests in room D200 alone. The

14 atmosphere in 200-rooms, where students get <u>tutored</u> and

15 make up tests, is less than ideal for this purpose. This

16 poses a problem: you may be taking a calculus test while

17 only ten feet away from you, well within hearing range, a

18 student is being tutored in geometry. Finally, the constant

19 noise of the copy machine <u>churning out</u> copies also is not

20 <u>conducive</u> to test taking.

21 We in no way mean to criticize the efforts of the

22 secretaries or teachers; it is not their fault. The problem

make up–take a test on a different day

block out–ignore

runs off–prints

gabbing–talking

? What problem is Erica writing about? (TONE)

tutored–taught personally

churning out–making quickly
conducive–favorable, good for

✎ Underline a fact Erica uses to support her opinion.

For use with Pupil's Edition pp. 446–453

CHAPTER 23

Worksheet A (cont.)   *Writing Workshop*

23 | is that there should be a designated room where students

24 | can make up tests or quizzes for any class. This room

25 | would be kept absolutely quiet and a test monitor could

26 | be <u>stationed</u> in the room to administer tests. Also, this   *stationed*–placed

27 | room could be open from 7:30 a.m. until 4:00 p.m.,

28 | giving students ample time to make up tests.

> ✎ **Underline the solution Erica proposes.**

29 | In the past, we have pointed out the need for a

30 | student lounge, but another problem in terms of space

31 | has <u>risen</u>. Students need a test make-up center, and we   *risen*–come up

32 | challenge the administration to find a room to set up this

33 | much-needed <u>facility</u>.   *facility*–place to work

CHAPTER 23

Worksheet B

Fill in the charts with information about the problems that interest you and their solutions. Use another sheet of paper if you need more space.

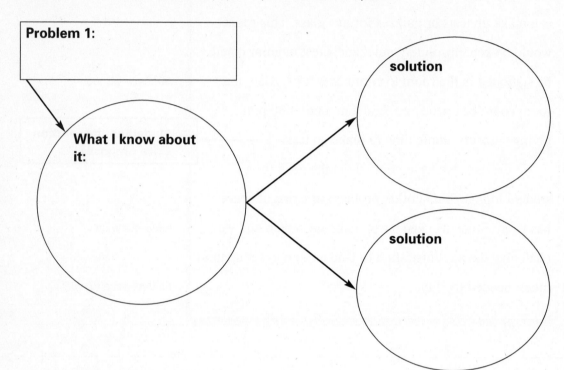

Problem 1:

What I know about it:

solution

solution

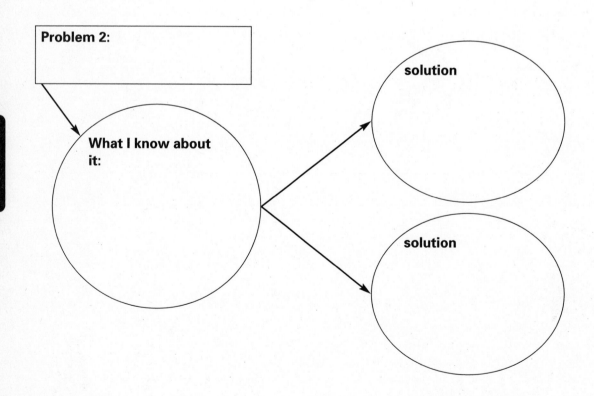

Problem 2:

What I know about it:

solution

solution

For use with Pupil's Edition pp. 446–453

Worksheet C

Writing Workshop

Answer the following questions about your problem. Use another sheet of paper if you need more space.

What is the problem? _____

_____

What do I want to happen?

_____

_____

What are the possible solutions?
Solution 1:

_____

_____

Solution 2:

_____

_____

Which solution do I like best?

_____

How will this solution work?

_____

_____

What facts, examples, quotes, or statistics show the problem or support the solution?

_____

_____

_____

CHAPTER 23

Worksheet D

Writing Workshop

Fill in the outline below to organize your writing. Take the information from
Worksheet C.

Introduction

The problem is:

_____

_____

The problem is important because:

_____

_____

Main Part

The problem is caused by:

_____

_____

These facts, examples, statistics, or quotes show that the problem is important:

_____

_____

The problem can be fixed by:

_____

_____

These facts, examples, statistics, or quotes show the solution will work:

_____

_____

Conclusion

In other words, the problem is important because:

_____

_____

The solution is:

_____

_____

CHAPTER 23

Copyright © McDougal Littell Inc.

For use with Pupil's Edition pp. 446–453

Worksheet E

Writing Workshop

Read the first draft of your writing. Then ask a friend to read it too. Discuss the following questions with your friend, and then write down the answers.

1. How can I state the problem more clearly?

_____

_____

_____

2. What more should I say about the problem? Would more information make it better?

_____

_____

_____

_____

3. What more should I say about the solution?

_____

_____

4. How can I change my writing to make it clearer?

_____

_____

_____

5. Do I talk about the problem and its solution in a clear and logical manner? What could I add to make my essay more interesting?

_____

_____

_____

6. Is my ending logical? How can I change my conclusion so that it summarizes the problem and its solution more clearly?

_____

_____

_____

_____

CHAPTER 23

Problem-Solution Essay

Background Information

This CD and the worksheets will take your students through the process of writing a problem-solution essay. In order to help students acquiring English succeed with this assignment, the process has been simplified.

Vocabulary for Problem-Solution Essay

You may wish to review the following words with your students before beginning this workshop. Refer to pages 7–9 for strategies for presenting vocabulary.

detail—a fact, an example, or another piece of information

essay—a short piece of writing that tells about a subject from the writer's personal point of view

solution—an answer; an explanation or a way of fixing a problem

example—an instance or illustration

freewrite—a way to explore ideas by writing whatever comes to your mind during a certain period of time

problem-solution essay—a description and the examination of a problem, with the proposal of one or more solutions to the problem

to solve—to explain, to find an answer to

to restate—to state again in a new form

Guiding Your Writers

See How It's Done

- Before students begin this workshop, introduce the problem-solution process with a brief discussion of a common school or neighborhood problem. Allow students to offer solutions and to share in evaluating them. Point out that this is the process they will follow as they write their essays.

- Before students read the essay "Test Center Needed" on Worksheet A, you may wish to review the vocabulary presented in the right margin. For strategies on how to present vocabulary effectively, refer to pages 7–9.

- To prepare students for reading this model, ask them to tell what they do not like about making up tests. After they complete their reading, ask them if they need help with any more words. Then ask them what they think of Erica's solution.

- **Worksheet A Possible answers:**

  ❓ **What problem is Erica writing about?** When you go to make up a test, you can't concentrate.

  ✎ **Underline a fact Erica uses to support her opinion.** Last semester, over 3,149 students had to make up tests in room D200 alone.

  ✎ **Underline the solution Erica proposes.** there should be a designated room where students can make up tests or quizzes for any class

Problem-Solution Essay

Do It Yourself

❶ Prewriting

• When students begin looking for writing ideas, you might suggest that they stay alert to problems they see about them every day on the way to school, at school, and in their neighborhood. Also encourage them to watch the news and read newspapers. They should keep a list of problems that interest them.

• After students have selected a problem to write about, you may wish to confer briefly with them. Check that their problems are suitable for the complexity of the essay they will be writing. You may want to help them focus on a more limited aspect of the problem. Also be sure that they have a definite solution in mind.

• To help students explore their ideas, you might encourage them to freewrite about their problems and solutions before completing Worksheet C.

• Encourage students to think about what causes the problem and how it affects them directly.

• Help students do their research. You may ask the school librarian to bring in books and magazines. It may be helpful to review how to look for information at the library and online.

• Discuss with students the plausibility of their solutions, how it would be implemented and by whom.

❷ Drafting

• Before students begin writing, look at their completed Worksheets C and D. Make sure they have a clear idea of the problem and enough information to explain the solutions they are proposing.

• Discuss with students the organization of their papers. Emphasize the need for a three-part essay and do a walk-through of what students should write in each part.

• The arguments students introduce should be logical. You may want to review cause-and-effect and sequential paragraphs from the thinking skills for writing at the beginning of the book. Discuss how these skills are helpful in writing problem-solution essays.

• Depending on their English proficiency, you may want to encourage students to use exact words, such as "students" instead of "people."

• If students have difficulty proceeding with the drafting stage, urge them to concentrate on getting their ideas down on paper without paying attention to vocabulary or grammar. They can correct and refine these aspects of writing as they revise and proofread.

CHAPTER 23

Problem-Solution Essay

❸ Revising ....

- Depending on the English proficiency of your students, you may wish to suggest one of the following formats for their writing:

Option 1
Ask students to write just one paragraph. In the first sentence, they should state the problem. They can tell why the problem is important and offer a solution in the following sentences of the paragraph.

Option 2
Have students write three paragraphs. In the first paragraph, they should identify the problem and tell why it is important. In paragraphs two and three, they should offer one or more solutions and explain how and why they would work.

Option 3
Have students develop longer essays of five to six paragraphs. The essays should follow a three-part organizational plan, with supporting details such as facts, examples, and statistics.

- Have students put their writing aside for a day or more, if possible, before they review it. As they discuss each other's writing, emphasize that the role of the peer reader at this stage is to comment solely on content and organization.

❹ Editing and Proofreading ....

- Explain to students that as writers they must decide which changes to make in their essays and that peer-reader comments are only suggestions.

- Depending on proficiency, you may want to have students check their essays for shifts in verb tenses.

- When students are ready to make their final copies, you may want to meet with them individually to explain the proofreading process you wish them to follow.

❺ Sharing and Reflecting ....

- To help students reflect more on their writing, ask what they learned about their topic while they gathered information and wrote their essay. Did anything surprise them? Encourage students to write their answers to these questions.

- Students may want to submit their essays for publication in local or school newspapers. They may also post their essays on the Internet.

- Review the skills and strategies the students used in examining and writing about a problem and solution. Point out that this type of writing is very useful in science, history, and other content areas. Ask students for examples of how it could be used in these subjects. Also explain how the skills learned by writing about a problem and solution will be helpful in other types of writing. For example, knowing how to examine and explain a problem will help them examine and explain a controversy or a cause-and-effect relationship.

CHAPTER 23

For use with Pupil's Edition pp. 446–453

Poetry

Writing Workshop

Each time you hear a tone (TONE), pause the CD and follow the instructions. Then restart the CD. Whenever you don't understand something, pause the CD and ask your teacher or a classmate to help you.

Getting Started

Writing a poem is like painting a picture. Instead of using brushes and paint, you use words. A **poem**, like a painting, shows what you think and feel. You do not have to use words that rhyme—that is, that end with the same sounds. You do not have to write about big ideas. You can use any words that you like, and you can write about anything that interests you.

- ◆ Turn to Worksheet A. Listen to the first poem that one student wrote and answer the question. Then, read the other poems on your own. Discuss the poems and the answers to the questions with your teacher and classmates. (TONE)

Now It's Your Turn

You will write a poem about something that is important to you. It can be about something very ordinary, or it might be about something you imagine or dream about.

❶ Prewriting ....

Find ideas for your poem.

Here are two ways to find ideas:

1. Make a list of special times in your life. Remember people, places, and events that were funny, sad, happy, or surprising. For example, you may remember your first night in a new home. You may remember a toy that you had long ago. You might remember a sad story that your grandmother told you.

2. What do you notice when you walk outside in the morning? What do you see, hear, and smell? What do you feel? Close your eyes and think for a minute. Then make a list. When you finish, share your list with your classmates.

   - ◆ Pause the CD and make your lists. (TONE)

Choose an idea and start working with it.

A subject is whatever a poem is about. Look at the ideas you wrote on your lists. Choose one idea for the subject of your poem. Then make some notes about your subject. Remember what it is like. Think about how you feel about it.

- ◆ After you choose a subject for your poem, fill in Worksheet B. Circle the words you like best. Then, show your notes to your teacher. (TONE)

Shape your poem.

You will write your poem in lines, not in sentences. A line might have one word, a few words, or many words. For example, see how Lauren writes the word "Earth" on line 60, and the words "in a cruel manner" on line 38. Candice chose to write many words on line 14, "Her fingers slowly sort through the faded pictures."

Look at the words you circled on Worksheet B. They will be part of your poem. Arrange these words in lines. Make each line show something about your subject.

CHAPTER 24

Poetry

Writing Workshop

As you work, think about the way your poem will look. You may use short lines, long lines, or some of each. Try more than one way to write your lines. Use Worksheet C to help you. If you have many long lines, try breaking some into shorter lines. If you have many short lines, try joining some to form longer lines. See which shape you like best. If you need a model, look at how Andrew shaped his poem on lines 1-11 on Worksheet A.

◆ On Worksheet C, write the lines of your poem in different ways. When you finish, show your work to your teacher. (TONE)

❷ Drafting ....

Write your poem.

Look at your work on Worksheet C. Choose the shape you like best, and write your poem again. This time, move, add, and change words to make your poem clearer. These three suggestions can help you write your poem:

1. Choose strong, exact words. Candice thought how beautiful and calm Mary looks. So she wrote "Shining, radiant, eternal." (line 30) Her words show exactly her impression of Mary.

2. Leave out words that you don't really need. For example, on line 22 Candice could have written "swimming in the river in July *to cool off from the heat,*" but everyone knows that swimming when it's hot is refreshing. She did not need to explain it.

3. The way a poem sounds is important. Say your poem aloud as you write, and listen to your words. Make your poem sound the way you want it to. You may want to repeat sounds. For example, Candice repeated the *f* sound in *fixes* (line 16) in *far* (line 17), *feuds* (line 18), and *friends* (line 19).

◆ Now write your poem. Use Worksheet C and the three suggestions above to help you. (TONE)

❸ Revising ....

Read your poem and think about it.

Read your poem to yourself. Then read it aloud to a classmate, and listen to your classmate's poem. Look at each other's poems and talk about them. Talk about what they are about, as well as how they sound.

◆ Share your poem with a classmate. (TONE)

Talk with your teacher about how you can change your poem. For more ideas, look again at Worksheets B and C. You might also read the poems on Worksheet A again. Then start making changes.

◆ Work with a classmate to write answers to the questions on Worksheet D. (TONE)

❹ Editing and Proofreading ....

Change your poem to make it better.

Keep working on your poem until you are happy with it. Proofread it as your teacher tells you to. Write your poem once more, putting in all your changes. Make your poem look as neat as possible.

◆ Make all the changes, and then write a final copy of your poem. (TONE)

For use with Pupil's Edition pp. 454–463

CHAPTER 24

Poetry

Writing Workshop

➎ Sharing and Reflecting ....

Share your poem with your classmates.

Your classmates and you may read your poems aloud. As you read, think about the emotions you are trying to share. Change your tone of voice and speed to show different emotions and make your reading more interesting to the audience.

Think about what you have learned.

When you write in a new way, you learn new things about writing and about yourself. Think about what you learned as you wrote your poem. How did your poem change as you worked on it? What did you like most about writing your poem?

◆ Think about these questions. Be ready to discuss your answers with your teacher and your classmates. (TONE)

CHAPTER 24

Worksheet A

Here are three poems written by students. As you read them, think about how
the writers show what they see and feel. Words that you may not understand
are underlined. They are explained on the right side of the page. Circle any other
words that you do not understand and ask your teacher what they mean.

Walking
by Andrew Love

1 I'm walking across the top of the <u>crusty</u> snow   *crusty*–hard

2   without falling through

3   without leaving footprints

4 without leaving any

5   <u>indication</u> that I was ever here at all.   *indication*–sign

6   But that's okay.

7 On the frozen snow that covers the ground

8   the walking is easier

9   if I take a little care

10   in where

11   I put my feet. |————————▶ **❓ What does the author describe? (TONE)**

Stories
by Candice Rhodes Mast

12 She sits

13 Bent over   *sort*–arrange, organize

14 Her fingers slowly <u>sort</u> through the faded pictures |—▶ **✏ Circle all the *s*- sounds in line 14.**

15 Telling her old stories again.

16 Her mind <u>fixes</u> on the black-and-white of   *fixes*–focuses, thinks about

17 <u>Far away</u> times   *Far away*–long ago, past

18 Long-ago <u>feuds</u>   *feuds*–fights

19 Old friends.

For use with Pupil's Edition pp. 454–463

CHAPTER 24

Worksheet A (cont.)

20	She is moving into her childhood world
21	Like a clock <u>wound</u> slowly backward.
22	Swimming in the river in July
23	Eating stolen watermelon
24	Coming home to find her <u>sweetheart</u>
25	Waiting on the porch.
26	"Quit running away from me, Mary," he said
27	And she did.
28	Soon she will come to the place where all
29	Life begins and ends,
30	Shining, <u>radiant</u>, eternal
31	She will turn to the angels and say,
32	"Let me tell you a story."

wound–turned

✏ **Underline one image Candice uses in lines 22–25.**

sweetheart–boyfriend

radiant–looking happy

How to Make a Sweet Potato Pie
by Lauren Hart

33	First, my child,
34	you must understand
35	the history of sweet potatoes.
36	Like our <u>ancestors</u>, they were
37	brought to this country
38	in a cruel manner,
39	<u>dredged</u> out of the dirt,
40	leaving many roots behind.
41	Picked <u>just short</u> of ripeness,
42	survivors of chilling nights
43	and hot, <u>parched</u> days,

ancestors–relatives from long ago

dredged–pulled

just short–just before

parched–hot and very dry

CHAPTER 24

Worksheet A (cont.)

Writing Workshop

44	they did not resist new <u>surroundings</u>;
45	instead, they <u>thrived</u>
46	with a unique style
47	and character.
48	They never forgot
49	where they came from.
50	Their master's stick
51	and shovel may have
52	dug into their sides
53	a hundred times,
54	but they never <u>faltered</u>,
55	never showed fear
56	or sadness.
57	No, child! They rose up
58	in grace and beauty
59	from their mother,
60	Earth.

surroundings–world around them
thrived–became strong

? **What does Lauren compare sweet potatoes to?**

faltered–stopped, tripped

CHAPTER 24

For use with Pupil's Edition pp. 454–463

Worksheet B

In the chart below, write about your subject. When you finish, circle the words that you like best.

Subject:
How does it look?
How does it sound?
If I touched it, what would my hand feel?
How does it smell?
How does it taste?
How do I feel about it?
What does it mean to me?

CHAPTER 24

Worksheet C

On a clean piece of paper, write the words that you circled on Worksheet C. Use them to write lines for your poem under "Shape 1" below. Under "Shape 2," use the same words to make lines of different lengths.

Shape 1

Shape 2

For use with Pupil's Edition pp. 454–463

Worksheet D

Together with a classmate, write answers to the questions below.

1. Which words could I change to show my subject more clearly?

_____

_____

_____

_____

2. What words could I add or change to show my feelings more clearly?

_____

_____

_____

_____

3. Which words could I take out without hurting the poem?

_____

_____

_____

_____

4. Which lines could be longer or shorter to make my poem better?

_____

_____

_____

_____

CHAPTER 24

Background Information

This CD and set of worksheets will guide students in composing poems. To make the workshop accessible to your students, discussions of figurative language and sound devices have been omitted from the lesson. The emphasis is on capturing sensory details and on communicating thoughts and feelings; students need not use rhyme or any fixed format.

Depending on your students' English proficiency, you may wish to introduce them to the processes of writing short stories and dramatic scenes as presented in the pupil's edition on pages 459–461. To do so, you may want to adapt some of the worksheets and suggestions detailed in this workshop.

Vocabulary for Poetry

Before students begin this workshop, make sure that they understand the following associated vocabulary. Refer to pages 7–9 for strategies to use in presenting vocabulary to your students.

poem—a kind of writing in which special forms and word sounds are used to help show feelings and ideas

to rhyme—to end with the same sounds

subject—what a poem is about

to break a line—to stop writing a line of poetry and begin a new line

Vocabulary for Extension

If you wish to introduce students to short story or dramatic scene writing, you might review the following terms.

plot—what happens in a story

characters—who is in a story

setting—where and when a story takes place

event—something that happens

first-person point of view—the telling of a story by a character in the story, using *I*

third-person point of view—the telling of a story by a storyteller who is not a character in the story

Guiding Your Writers

See How It's Done

- You might let students know that most poems go through numerous drafts. Explain that in this assignment they will rewrite their poems several times, making changes and trying various formats.

- You may wish to point out that although some English poems use end rhymes, many others do not. To be sure that students know what rhyming words are, you might offer examples, such as *cat* and *rat*. Reassure students that their poems need not rhyme.

For use with Pupil's Edition pp. 454–463

Poetry

- Before students read the models you may wish to discuss what they know about poems and which poems or authors they may be familiar with. Invite students to talk about works in their own language.

- Have students read the models: first silently to themselves, then aloud as a group, then silently to themselves once more.

- After students read the models, you might open a discussion by asking how each poem helps them to "see" the details the author describes. Encourage them to identify the lines that give them clear mental pictures. Then ask how they think the writer feels about his or her subject. Ask which parts of the poem show the writer's feelings. Point out that the writers do not state their feelings directly; rather, they describe details in a way that shows their feelings. Suggest that students use a similar technique in their poems.

- **Worksheet A Possible answers:**

  ❓ What does the author describe? walking on the snow

  ✎ Circle all the *s*- sounds in line 14. fingers; slowly; sort; pictures

  ✎ Underline one image Candice uses in lines 22–25. Swimming in the river in July; Eating stolen watermelon; Coming home to find her sweetheart

  ❓ What does Lauren compare sweet potatoes to? our ancestors

Do It Yourself

❶ Prewriting ....

- The first option can be used as a group activity. Have students sit in a circle and pass around a piece of paper with "I remember" written at the top. Each student should write at least one thing that he or she remembers. To stimulate ideas, you might add the headings "People," "Places," and "Events." Encourage students to list items under each heading.

- You might invite students to use sketching to find ideas. Suggest that they sketch objects that they see every day. To increase language use, have students trade their sketches and discuss them. Then have them freewrite their thoughts and feelings about their sketches. Ask them to underline the parts of their freewriting that give them ideas for poems.

- If a student is finding it difficult to choose a subject, suggest that the student begin writing poems about two subjects. The subject for which he or she can generate more material will be the one to develop.

❷ Drafting ....

- To help students understand how line breaks can affect a poem, you might write the first model on the board, combining several of the shorter lines. Invite students to discuss the effects of the new line breaks. Some students may find that longer lines make the poem seem more complex or harder to follow; others may feel that longer lines flow better. Stress the idea that there is no "right" way to break lines of poetry, and that writers can please their own ears and eyes.

CHAPTER 24

Poetry

- You may wish to point out that one way to emphasize a word or phrase is to place it at the end or the beginning of a line.

- You might suggest one of the following options to each student, depending on his or her English proficiency:

Option 1

The student turns in Worksheets B and C, carefully completed.

Option 2

The student turns in a draft of a poem based on material from Worksheet C. The draft should include sensory details and should show attention to line breaks.

Option 3

The student expands on Option 2 by turning in two or more drafts of the same poem, each of which includes changes to make the subject and tone clearer, the wording more exact, and the sound devices more effective.

- To encourage students to use concrete, sensory details in their poems, you might introduce the idea of "Show, don't tell." Ask students to find places in the model where the authors show instead of telling.

❸ Revising

- For tips on pairing your students for peer response and on creating a supportive classroom atmosphere, see pages 4–6.

- Check each student's completed copy of Worksheets C and D.

- Depending on students' English proficiency, you may wish to point out that punctuation can be used to increase a poem's clarity. You might guide individual students in using commas and end marks as needed.

- When students are ready to begin their final drafts, meet with them individually and explain the proofreading process you want each student to follow. Various approaches to proofreading are described on pages 12–13.

❹ Editing and Proofreading

- Depending on students' English proficiency, you may wish to point out that figurative language can be used to increase a poem's capacity to convey images. You might guide individual students in using the forms of figurative language outlined in the student text on page 457.

❺ Sharing and Reflecting

- You might have students share their final drafts with the peers who saw the earlier drafts. Encourage peers to comment on changes.

- To help students reflect on their writing processes, you might have them respond in writing to the questions. You may also ask the following questions, What parts of your poem are you now most—and least—satisfied with? How is writing a poem like other kinds of writing? How is it different?

- Students may wish to illustrate their poems and gather them in a class book.

For use with Pupil's Edition pp. 454–463

CHAPTER 24

Research Report

Writing Workshop

Each time you hear a tone (TONE), pause the CD and follow the instructions. Then restart the CD and keep listening. When anything is unclear, pause and replay a part of the CD. You might also ask your teacher or another student for help.

See How It's Done

Think back to the first time you heard about an interesting subject. How did you learn more about it? What did you think after you learned more about it? By writing a **research report**, you will learn more about a subject that interests you. Then, you will share what you think about it.

◆ Now turn to Worksheet A and listen to the beginning of a research report one student wrote. Answer the question, and then pause the CD. Continue to read the report and answer the questions. (TONE)

Do It Yourself

You will write a research report about a subject that interests you. It could be anything you are interested in, such a hobby, a sport, an animal, a person, or an object.

❶ Developing a Research Plan ....

Find something to write about.

On a sheet of paper, list things that you would like to know more about. You might list sports, hobbies, authors, and historical or current events. Look at your list and choose the subject that you find the most interesting. Circle it and write why you think this topic is interesting.

◆ Make your list, and then choose a topic. (TONE)

Think about what you need to know.

Use Worksheet B to write what you already know about your subject and what you need to learn about it. Ask yourself these questions: Where did it come from? Who started it? How did it become what it is now? Was any research done about this subject? What do I want to learn about it? Circle the questions that are the most interesting to you. You may use the answers later in your report. Think about where you can look for the answers to your questions.

◆ Fill out Worksheet B. Talk about your ideas with your teacher. (TONE)

Start gathering information.

Now you can start looking for the answers to your questions. Use Worksheet C to decide where you will look for the information you need.

◆ Pause the CD. Fill out Worksheet C. (TONE)

Make sure that the source of information is useful.

Look at the date of the resource. Information that is old may no longer be correct. For example, research that was done ten years ago may not be correct any more. Look at who wrote the information. Does the author know a lot about the subject? Try to use as many different sources as possible. This will give you different points of view and more ideas to choose from.

◆ Now look for the information you need. (TONE)

CHAPTER 25

Research Report

❷ Using and Documenting Sources ....

Find and write the answers to your questions.

You need to write down the information that answers your questions as well as other important details you find about your subject. Here are three ways to help you do this:

1. First, look through your list of sources. Read what you wrote on Worksheet C. Then decide which sources are the best. After reading your list, you might decide that some sources may not be available to you, or that some may be more useful.

2. If you think the source is useful, look for the information you need. You need to write where exactly you read each piece of information so you can find it again.

3. Check your sources. For each source, ask yourself the following questions: How old is the information? Does the source list an author? Who is the author? Does the author know a lot on this subject? What is the author's point of view? What might influence the author's opinion?

   ◆ Pause the CD and decide which sources of information you will use.

❸ Taking Notes ....

Use index cards to record your information.

Write all the information on index cards. Use separate cards for each source of information.

1. Write where the information comes from (book, magazine, Internet), its title, author, date, and any other useful details that will help you or someone else find it again. If you get information from the Internet, you must also write down the name and address of the site and the date when you accessed it.

2. Take notes: write every new fact and detail you find about your topic. Write the page number where you found the information.

3. Summarize the main idea. Write the main idea of the piece of information in your own words, in a clear and brief way. Add only the most important supporting details. When you write an author's ideas in your own words, you paraphrase the author. It is not the same as copying what an author says. When you copy an author's words, you must use quotation marks to let your readers know that these are not your own words.

4. Include interesting quotes on your cards. Remember to add quotation marks.

5. Number your cards in the order you write them.

   ◆ Now turn to Worksheet D. Use index cards to write down your information. (TONE)

❹ Crafting a Good Thesis Statement ....

Think about the main idea of your report.

Now that you have done all your research, you are ready to begin your report. A good way to start is to write down the main idea, or thesis statement, of your paper. The thesis statement tells what you think of your subject. You should base your thesis statement on what you know and what you have found out during your research.

(**For use with Pupil's Edition pp. 464–479**)

Research Report

For example, Sandra wanted to examine the question of whether or not animals use language to communicate. Her thesis was that animals may have language skills, even if they can't talk. In her report, she used the information she found to back up her thesis statement.

◆ Now think about your thesis statement. Write it on a piece of paper and choose note cards that will back it up. (TONE)

❺ Organizing and Outlining ....

Organize the information.

Think about how you will organize your report. The first thing you need to do is to sort your index cards in different groups. Put cards with information about one key idea in the same group.

For example, Sandra may have put cards about the theories on language in one group and cards about research on the language skills of chimpanzees in another.

◆ Sort your information cards. (TONE)

Create an outline.

The outline is the skeleton of your report. It is a way of putting in order what you will write about. To make your outline, first write down your subject. Then, write your thesis statement. Next, look at your groups of cards. Name the key idea of each group. One of Sandra's key ideas was that language may exist without speech. Write your key ideas on Worksheet E.

Next, you need to add details that support each key idea. Copy important details and quotes from your note cards in the spaces below each key idea.

◆ Now complete Worksheet E. (TONE)

❻ Drafting ....

Now draft your research report.

Now you are ready to draft your report. Review your index cards and the outline you created on Worksheet E. As you write, keep in mind that the goal of your report is to support and share your thesis statement. Remember that a draft is not a finished piece of writing. You may change it many times before you are happy with it.

◆ Now begin drafting your research report. (TONE)

❼ Documenting Information ....

You need to identify all your sources of information in the text, and then write a list of your sources.

1. To do this, first include some information in parentheses next to each quoted phrase. For example, on lines 31–34, Sandra writes, "Chimpanzees do travel down the language road given the appropriate rearing environment, but they travel more slowly than humans, and not as far" (Savage-Rumbaugh and Lewin 177–178). The parentheses tell the reader the name of the author and the page number where the information can be found. If the source has no author, write the topic and page number. To refer to sources such as dictionaries, encyclopedies, or almanacs, write the title or the source, such as Encyclopaedia Britannica Online on line 3 of Worksheet A.

CHAPTER 25

Research Report

2. After the text, list all the sources you refer to in your paper in alphabetical order. First write the name of the author, the title, the place and the name of the publisher, the date it was published, and the page number where you found the information. See how Sandra listed her sources in lines 41–62 of Worksheet A.

◆ Now write the list of works you quote in your report. (TONE)

❽ Revising ....

Read over what you have written.

You might want to ask your teacher or a friend to suggest changes for your paper. Remember that your goal is to support and share your thesis.

◆ Turn to Worksheet F. Discuss the questions with your teacher or a friend. Write down your answers. Then show your completed work to your teacher. (TONE)

❾ Editing and Proofreading ....

Continue changing your writing until you are happy with it.

Make sure you have used punctuation marks correctly in your report. You may want to ask your teacher or a friend to help you. Then, check to be sure you listed your sources correctly. Look on page 476 of your textbook to learn how to give your sources in the report. You might also ask your teacher for more advice on how to proofread your writing.

◆ Proofread your writing, and then make a clean copy. (TONE)

❿ Sharing and Reflecting ....

Think about what you have learned by doing this writing.

Share your writing with your teacher and classmates. Ask them what they learned from reading your report. Then, discuss the following questions: What would you do differently next time? What did you learn about your subject? What did you learn about doing research? How can you use what you have learned in other classes? Place your index cards, the outline, and your report in your Working Portfolio.

◆ Share your report with a classmate, and then answer the questions. (TONE)

(For use with Pupil's Edition pp. 464–479)

Worksheet A

Below is a research report that one student wrote about the language skills of animals. As you read the report, notice how Sandra Williams writes and uses the information she found about language and animal communication. Think about how it helps you understand what she thinks about the language skills of animals. Words that you may not know are underlined and are explained on the right side of the page. Circle any other words that you don't know and ask your teacher or a classmate for help.

Do Animals Possess Language?
by Sandra Williams

1 Do animals communicate through language? The

2 answer may depend on how language is defined.

3 According to <u>Encyclopaedia Britannica Online</u>, language

4 is "a system of <u>conventional</u> spoken or written symbols

5 by means of which human beings. . . communicate."

6 According to this definition, animals do not (and cannot)

7 have language. Yet <u>recent</u> research suggests that some

8 animals do possess language skills, despite the fact that

9 they do not speak.

10 Is <u>speech</u> a necessary part of language? Professor

11 Philip Lieberman of Brown University writes that speech

12 is "one of the key elements, if not <u>the</u> key element, in

13 fully developed human language and <u>cognition</u>" (150).

14 This would seem to disqualify animals as users of

15 language. On the other hand, Dr. E. Sue Savage-

16 Rumbaugh <u>claims</u> that understanding language is an

17 important element too.

18 In her research, Savage-Rumbaugh has demonstrated

19 that chimpanzees can be taught to understand human

20 speech. In one study, Savage-Rumbaugh compared the

conventional–traditional, accepted

recent–just done, almost new

✎ **Underline Sandra's thesis statement.** (TONE)

speech–ability to talk

cognition–the ability to learn

claims–says, states as true

✎ **Circle the question Sandra is trying to answer in this paragraph.**

CHAPTER 25

Worksheet A (cont.)

Writing Workshop

21 language <u>comprehension</u> of a one-and-a-half-year-old

22 human child named Alia and an eight-year-old ape named

23 Kanzi. Each <u>responded</u> to hundreds of sentences spoken

24 in English (Savage-Rumbaugh et al. 45). While both

25 showed that they understood most of the sentences, Kanzi,

26 the chimp, <u>outscored</u> Alia by 72% to 66% overall (76).

27   Savage-Rumbaugh has concluded that a chimpanzee

28 can <u>acquire</u> language skills similar to those of a two-

29 year-old child if both the child and the chimp are raised

30 in a "language-rich environment." She writes,

31 "Chimpanzees do travel down the language road given

32 the appropriate <u>rearing</u> environment, but they travel more

33 slowly than humans, and not as far" (Savage-Rumbaugh

34 and Lewin 177–78).

35   Other research provides evidence that animals may

36 be physically able to <u>possess</u> language skills. According

37 to a 1998 <u>Science</u> article, researchers have discovered

38 that a language area of the brain that was once thought to

39 be unique to humans is also present in chimpanzees

40 (Gannon et al. 220).

41   **Works <u>Cited</u>**

42 Anger, Natalie. "Chimpanzee Doin' What Comes

43   Culturally." <u>New York Times</u>

44   17 June 1999: A=1+.

comprehension–
understanding

responded–answered

✎ **Circle the statistic Sandra uses to support her thesis statement.**

acquire–get, learn

rearing–raising (a child),
training as you grow up

✎ **Circle the source of information Sandra quotes in this paragraph.**

possess–have

Cited–from which quotations were taken

❓ **In which newspaper was this article published? Who wrote it?**

For use with Pupil's Edition pp. 464–479

CHAPTER 25

Worksheet A (cont.)

45   Gannon, Patrick J., et al. "Asymmetry of Chimpanzee

46   Planum Temporale: Humanlike Pattern of Wernicke's

47   Brain Language Area Homolog." <u>Science</u> 9 Jan.

48   1998: 220–22.

49   Golden, Frederic. "Clever Kanzi." <u>Discover</u> Mar. 1991: 20.

50   "Language." <u>Encyclopaedia Britannica Online</u>, vers. 99.1.

51   Encylopaedia Britannica. 23 Mar. 1999

52   <http://www.eb.com:180/bol/topic?

53   ea=114866&sctn=1>.

54   Lieberman, Philip. <u>Eve Spoke</u>: <u>Human Language and

55   Human Evolution</u>. New York: Norton, 1998.

56   Savage-Rumbaugh, E. Sue, et al. <u>Language

57   Comprehension in Ape and Child</u>. Monographs of

58   the Society for Research in Child Development, 58,

59   3–4. Chicago: Chicago, 1993.

60   Savage-Rumbaugh, Sue, and Roger Lewin. <u>Kanzi: The

61   Ape at the Brink of the Human Mind</u>. New York:

62   Wiley, 1994.

Worksheet B

Writing Workshop

Subject: _____

Why I like this subject: _____

What I already know about my subject:

What I need to find out about my subject:

CHAPTER 25

Worksheet C

Write which information you can find in the sources listed.

Library

_____

_____

_____

Encyclopedia

_____

_____

_____

Dictionary

_____

_____

_____

Books

_____

_____

_____

Magazines

_____

_____

_____

Internet

_____

_____

_____

Other

_____

_____

CHAPTER 25

Worksheet D

Writing Workshop

Look how Sandra filled out the first card. Fill out the second card with one of your information sources. Then take notes on your own index cards as you research. Fill as many cards as you need. You can copy the information you wrote on this sheet on a separate index card.

type of work　　　　　　**index card number**

Book　　　　　　　　　　　　　　　　　1

author(s)

Lieberman, Philip

title

Eve Spoke: Human Language and　　　New York: Norton, 1998
Human Evolution.

• place of publisher
• name of publisher
• date of publication

main idea(s) in your own words

Since chimpanzees can't talk, they can't develop or have language.

quote

[speech] "is one of the key elements, if not the key element, in fully developed human language and cognition"
Professor Philip Lieberman - Brown University - page 150

author of the quote　　　**other information/details**

_____　　　　　　　　　　　　　_____

_____

_____　　_____

_____

_____

_____

_____

For use with Pupil's Edition pp. 464–479

CHAPTER 25

Worksheet E

Complete this worksheet to create an outline for your research report. Depending on your subject, you may not be able to fill out every line, or you may need to add other lines. You may use a separate sheet of paper to create your outline.

I. Introduction
    My subject is:

    _____

    _____

    My thesis statement is:

    _____

    _____

    _____

II. Key Idea 1: _____

    Detail 1 _____

    Detail 2 _____

    Detail 3 _____

III. Key Idea 2: _____

    Detail 1 _____

    Detail 2 _____

    Detail 3 _____

IV. Key Idea 3: _____

    Detail 1 _____

    Detail 2 _____

    Detail 3 _____

Worksheet F

Read over the first draft of your writing and share it with a friend. Then, discuss the following questions and write down your answers.

1. Is my thesis statement clear? How can I make my introduction more interesting?

_____

_____

2. What examples, details, or quotes can I add to better support my thesis statement?

_____

_____

_____

_____

3. How can I improve the organization of my report? Which information could be added or left out?

_____

_____

_____

_____

4. Do the quotes help understand the main ideas that I am explaining?

_____

_____

_____

_____

5. Did I include a list at the end that tells where I found each piece of information or quote I wrote? Is this list in the correct format?

_____

_____

_____

_____

For use with Pupil's Edition pp. 464–479

Research Report

Background Information

In order to adapt this Writing Workshop to accommodate your students' knowledge of English, the number of options presented at various stages in the writing process has been limited. For example, students are led to make singular source cards and only one organizational strategy is explained.

The suggestions that follow are related to the instructions for writing a research report that appear in the audiotape script.

Vocabulary for Research Report

You may wish to review the following words with your students before teaching this workshop. You will find suggestions for presenting vocabulary on pages 7–9 of this booklet.

detail—a small part of something, a small piece of information

thesis statement—a sentence that tells the main idea of a paper

to paraphrase—to write an author's ideas in another way, with your own words

subject—a topic, a thing being discussed

quotation—repeating a passage or word from a piece of literature

information source—place, such as a book, a magazine, or Internet site, where you get facts and details that support the main idea

Guiding Your Writers

See How It's Done

- To prepare students to read the model on Worksheet A, invite them to share what they know about how animals communicate. Do they think animals "talk" to each other? How?

- **Worksheet A Possible answers:**

  - **Underline Sandra's thesis statement.** Yet recent research suggests that some animals do possess language skills, despite the fact that they do not speak.

  - **Circle the question Sandra is trying to answer in this paragraph.** Is speech a necessary part of language?

  - **Circle the statistic Sandra uses to support her thesis statement.** Kanzi, the chimp, outscored Alia by 72% to 66% overall.

  - **Circle the source of information Sandra quotes in this paragraph.** (Savage-Rumbaugh and Lewin 177–78)

  - **In which newspaper was this article published?** in the New York Times **Who wrote it?** Natalie Anger

CHAPTER 25

Personal Narrative

Do It Yourself

❶ Developing a Research Plan ....

- Help students determine if their subjects are appropriate. If a student chooses a term that is too broad, such as music, suggest that he or she make a cluster to break the topic down into more specific terms, like *rock*, *jazz*, *reggae*, and *rap*.

- You might ask your school librarian to bring in books and periodicals that students can use to research their topics. It may be helpful to review how to look for a dictionary or encyclopedia entry, log on the Internet, or find a call number.

❷ Using and Documenting Sources ....

- Students may want to photocopy longer articles in order to highlight the main ideas before summarizing them on their cards.

❸ Taking Notes ....

- Encourage students to write down statistics, quotations, and other pertinent material. You may want to emphasize the difference between paraphrasing and plagiarizing. Explain that each time they use an author's exact words, no matter how many, they need to use quotation marks and attribute the quote.

❹ Crafting a Good Thesis Statement ....

- Remind students that their thesis statements should reflect their opinions about the subjects they chose. Students should think about what information will support their thesis. Some students may need help to narrow their subjects or find a better angle. Encourage students to write their thesis statements in a clear and brief way. Then meet with students individually to review and discuss their thesis statements.

- Encourage students to ask the following questions about their thesis: Will my readers understand what I mean? How much research will this subject need? Is my subject clearly stated?

❺ Organizing and Outlining ....

- Make sure that students understand the purpose of an outline. Invite them to think about how they would start writing their essays without making an outline first. Explain that the outline helps them decide how they will arrange the information in order to support their thesis statements in a logical and effective manner.

- You may want to refer them to the model on page 473 of their textbooks and discuss how the outline helped Sandra write her essay. Have students think about why Sandra chose this outline and what else she could have done.

❻ Drafting ....

- Meet with each student before he or she begins drafting. Depending on the student's English proficiency, you may wish to suggest one of the following three options:

For use with Pupil's Edition pp. 464–479

Research Report

Option 1
Students write one paragraph in which they state the subject and the thesis statement and include two references to information sources.

Option 2
Students choose a subject, do research, record the information on index cards and write a detailed outline.

Option 3
Students research a topic of their choice and make an outline. Students then write a report with a least one paragraph for each part of the outline, including quotes and references to their information sources.

❼ Documenting Information

- Meet with students individually to help them format their Work Cited lists at the end of their reports. You may want to use Worksheet A as a model. You may also review page 476 of the textbook with students.

- Remind students that common knowledge, such as "chimpanzees can't talk" need not be attributed.

❽ Revising

- Suggest that each student ask his or her readers to summarize what they learned about the subject of the report and if the report helps them understand the main ideas.

- Suggest the strategy of putting the work aside for a few hours or a day. When students read it again, they will have a fresher perspective.

- Encourage students to review the placement and punctuation of each quote they used. How does the quote help understand the idea developed in the sentence? Is the full quote needed or would part of the quote be enough?

- Remind students that they should feel free to ask you or a classmate for suggestions on how to improve their writing.

❾ Editing and Proofreading

- You may wish to tailor the proofreading requirements to accommodate each student's proficiency level. See pages 12–13 for options you might use. Depending on proficiency, you may want to focus on one type of error, such as punctuating correctly parenthetical information in the Works Cited list.

❿ Sharing and Reflecting

- Review the skills students have used in their writing and discuss how they might be applicable to other types of writing and other curricular areas. Have students record their answers and include them in their Working Portfolios along with their outlines, index cards, and finished research reports.

- Encourage students to bring visual aids, such as photos or graphics, to show their classmates as they share their finished papers. They may want to post their reports on the Internet.

CHAPTER 25

Thinking Skills Answer Key

Page 17 Writing Process
c, e, b, d, f, a

Page 18 Sequential Paragraph
1. c, d, b, a
2. b, e, d, c, a

Page 19 Cause and Effect Paragraph
1. d, c, a, e, b
2. d, a, f, e, c, b

Page 20 Comparison-Contrast Paragraph
1. c, f, b, a, d, e
2. a, d, f, c, e, b

Page 21 Five-Paragraph Composition
d, c, b, e, a

Page 22 Introductions
1. c, b, a
2. b, c, a
3. b, d, c, a

Page 23 Conclusions
1. b, c, a
2. b, c, a
3. a, c, b

Page 24 Adding Factual Elaboration to a Paragraph
Possible Answers:
1. <u>A Russian-American scientist called Vladimir Zworykin</u> helped create television in the 1920s. (d)
2. But broadcasting did not begin in the U.S. until <u>after the Second World War.</u> (c)
3. Then, scientists made television better <u>by making color TVs and introducing cable access.</u> (e)
4. Today, <u>97 million homes in America</u> have at least one TV set. (a)
5. There are even two Museums of Television and Radio<u>, one in Los Angeles, the other in New York City</u>. (b)

Page 25 Adding Sensory Elaboration to a Paragraph
Possible Answers:
1. When the movie begins, we hear thunder <u>clapping violently in the night sky</u>. (d)
2. Then, we see Count Dracula's castle <u>perched on top of a steep, bare mountain</u>. (b)
3. A young man <u>wearing a soft silk cape and rich leather boots</u> is riding a horse up the mountain. (a)
4. At dinner, the young man won't eat his soup <u>because it smells like rotten eggs.</u> (e)

5. As the movie goes on, the young man <u>becomes wrinkled and his hair thins and grays.</u> (c)

Page 26 Adding Incidents, Examples, Quotations
Possible Answers:
1. c, 2. b, 3. a

Page 27 Combining Short Sentences
1. Juan likes all kinds of movies<u>, but</u> his favorites are westerns.
2. He started to watch every western on TV <u>after</u> he saw his first western and loved it.
3. They don't make many westerns these days<u>, so</u> he rents videos.
4. Juan doesn't really like westerns in black and white <u>because</u> they look so much better in color.

Page 28 Combining Sentences Using Words, Phrases, Appositives
Possible Answers:
1. <u>My best friend</u> Felipe is always telling jokes.
2. He started to tell a joke <u>yesterday morning.</u>
3. The joke was about a chicken <u>hopping backwards.</u>
4. He was about to tell <u>why the chicken was hopping backwards.</u>
5. Just then, Mr. Hernandez<u>, our coach,</u> called us to the gym.

Page 29 Placement of Modifiers
Possible Answers:
1. An insect's body is made up of three <u>different</u> parts: the head, the thorax, and the abdomen.
2. Insects <u>always</u> have six legs and two antennae.
3. They use their <u>sensitive</u> antennae to feel the world around them.
4. Some insects, including flies and bees, have <u>four</u> wings.
5. A few types of insects have created <u>very</u> complex societies.

Page 30 Inverted Sentences
1. Has Maria seen the movie you are talking about?
2. Is that movie very scary?
3. Were the characters really lost in the woods?
4. Were they looking for an old cave?
5. Did they get very scared?
6. Did they find their way out?
7. Do you think the actors will win Oscars?